Jndn Hallent CATALONIA

20/9/93
The Vineyard Wine Club
Belfast

Jan Read and Maite Manjón

CATALONIA
Traditions, places, wine and food

The Herbert Press

In memory of Miguel Torres Carbó, winemaker extraordinary

First published in Great Britain 1992
by The Herbert Press Ltd, 46 Northchurch Road, London N1 4EJ

Designed by Pauline Harrison
House editor Brenda Herbert
Cartographer John Flower
Set in 10/12pt Lectura by Nene Phototypesetters Ltd, Northampton
Printed and bound in Hong Kong by South China Printing
Company (1988) Ltd

A CIP catalogue record for this book is available from the
British Library.

ISBN 1-871569-42-7

Front cover illustration: The Monastery of Sant Pere de Rodes.
Photo: Tor Eigeland

Frontispiece: Detail of the carving on the facade of the Sagrada
Família

Contents

Acknowledgements

First and foremost we should like to thank Miguel A. Torres, who first suggested that we should write this book with the object of interesting readers and visitors in the many fascinating aspects of Catalonia, not least its wines and cuisine. Miguel Torres SA has made a major contribution towards producing the book and we are grateful to their staff for practical help on the ground, and for the use of the illustration on p.145.

We are also grateful to Marimar Torres for allowing us to reproduce the recipe on p.214 from her book *The Spanish Table*, to Irene and Andreu España of Casa Irene at Arties for the recipe on p.221 and to Jaume Subirós of the Hotel-Restaurant Ampurdán, both for leave to print his recipes on pp.204 and 221 and for a great deal of fascinating information on Catalan cooking.

Parts of Chapter IV on *cava* and the Penedès have previously appeared in the Boston *Quarterly Review of Wines*.

Our thanks go to Waltraud Torres for permission to reproduce her beautiful painting on pp.158–9. Codorníu SA kindly allowed us to reproduce the posters and the photograph on pp.150 and 151, and Freixenet SA the Miró drawing on p.154. The intriguing poster on p.187 is included by permission of Casa Riera Ordeix of Vic, and the photograph of nuts on p.182 by permission of ICEX, Madrid. The photograph on the cover was taken specially for this book by Tor Eigeland.

All the other photographs in the book were taken by Jan Read.

Foreword

My first visit to Catalonia was to Tossa de Mar when James Mason and Ava Gardner were filming that eccentric epic about a ghostly sea captain and his ship, *Pandora and the Flying Dutchman*. In those distant days, Tossa boasted four small family hotels, a fishermen's bar and another bar run by a buccaneer with a gold tooth. The fishing boats were drawn up the length of the crescent-shaped beach and put out each night with great gas-lit globes over the stern, distancing themselves from the shore and looking in the end like a row of lamp-posts on the horizon. Sometimes in the morning a boat would tow out a long net and a party on the beach would haul it in by the ends, anyone who had helped being entitled to part of the silvery mound of small fish.

I [J.R.] grew very attached to Tossa, to picnics by donkey cart and *paellas* cooked in the open air or excursions further afield along villainously pot-holed roads in an ancient Erskine automobile (the only car for hire and of a make I have never heard of before or since) to unspoilt towns and villages like Santa Coloma de Farners or Hostalric. On my last visit I presented my guide and friend, Rafael Toscano, with a set of Linguaphone records with which he organized sessions to teach the villagers English. That, in hindsight, was a small part of the beginning of the end.

Although much of that rocky and beautiful coast remains as it was, the Costa Brava was among the first parts of Spain to be overwhelmed by mass tourism. The pity is that of the millions of foreign visitors who have crowded its beaches, and later those of Salou and the Costa Daurada, not many realize that Catalonia has so much else to offer. And this is a point worth making with millions more thronging into Barcelona for the 1992 Olympic Games.

A great deal has happened since the Royal Decree of 29 September 1977 re-established Catalonia's historic parliament, the Generalitat, and restored a large measure of autonomy to the country. It is not simply the signs on the roads or public notices, now written in Catalan in preference to the Spanish of Castile, which have changed. There is a resurgence of pride in things Catalan: in the history of a kingdom that was once a great seafaring power and mistress of the Mediterranean; in art,

literature and the architecture of an innovator such as Gaudí; in industry, where Barcelona has often led Spain; in the diversity of its wines and in the rediscovery and renaissance of the native cuisine.

For the visitor, Catalonia is, to begin with, a country for people who like the open air — whether for scenery or participation in outdoor pursuits. We suggest that you do not miss the jutting forelands, the turquoise water and the secret coves and beaches of the Costa Brava; the wooded mountains and unspoilt towns and villages of the Serra de Montseny; the Catalan Pyrenees, white and majestic in winter, and with valleys carpeted with flowers in spring and summer; the high valley of the Ebro and the Serra de Caballs, with narrow roads winding through plum, cherry and peach orchards, and a view of some lost terracotta township and blue mountains in the distance; or, as a contrast, the pancake flatness of the Ebro delta, its paddy fields and wild-life preserve beyond Tortosa.

If you are a fisherman, you will make for the trout streams of the Pyrenees, and there is spear and deep-sea fishing in the Mediterranean; sailing is a ruling passion in Catalonia, and there are marinas and port facilities all along the three hundred miles of coastline; climbers and hikers are well provided for, with serious mountaineering in the Pyrenees and a multitude of trails, sometimes with simple refuges and cooking facilities, in the Pyrenees and its foothills, the Serra de Montseny and other mountain areas; rough shooting is popular and permits can be obtained from local hunting and fishing associations; and from December to April there is first-rate skiing in the Vall d'Aran, La Cerdanya and the Vall de Ter, with well-maintained pistes, scores of ski lifts, good hotels and restaurants and all the resort amenities.

As in the rest of Spain the many festivals are an attraction. Some, like the Easter processions, the celebration of St George's Day (Sant Jordi is the patron saint of Catalonia as well as of England) with bouquets of roses, or the noisy devil dances and dragons, take place up and down Catalonia. Many other festivals are local: each town or village has its own saint and sets aside a day to honour him. These festivities often feature huge, grotesquely painted papier maché giants (*gegants*) or *castells*, human towers of young men in national costume; and at each and every festival you will always see a circle of *sardana* dancers. *Sardana* dancing is a national pastime.

The most lasting reward of a visit to any unfamiliar country is to come away with a deepened knowledge and understanding of its people and traditions, and in Catalonia the physical remains are all around. Empúries, with its mosaics and broken columns beside the blue sea and sandy pinewoods of the Gulf of Roses, was a Greek settlement three centuries before the Romans landed there. Tarragona evokes Roman power at its height, with its massive walls, amphitheatre, praetorium and splendid aqueduct. Especially in the mountainous north, the Roman influence survives in the numerous Romanesque churches, and across Catalonia as a whole there are some two thousand buildings in this architectural style. Medieval Catalonia is represented by monasteries such as Sant Pere de Rodes, Poblet and Santes Creus; by splendid Gothic cathedrals, like those of Girona and Tarragona; and by the ruined castles still keeping watch from the hilltops. Equally evocative of another era is another cathedral, Gaudí's masterpiece, the as yet uncompleted Sagrada Família in Barcelona, with its soaring towers and convoluted sculpture.

It has been said that Barcelona *is* Catalonia. Certainly it is one of the liveliest and most handsome of European cities and typifies the energy, drive and self-confidence of the Catalans. Here you will find spacious tree-lined boulevards with elegant shops and, as a contrast, the characterful old streets of the Gothic Quarter, the Cathedral and historic parliament building, the Generalitat, and the Ramblas with its flower stalls. There is a superb museum of early Catalan art and galleries devoted to Picasso and Miró; the Liceu is one of the finest opera houses in Europe; and the city possesses many of the most innovative restaurants in Spain and the kinkiest of nightspots open until all hours.

Practicalities

GEOGRAPHY

Catalonia is divided into four provinces: Lleida (Lérida) and Girona (Gerona) in the north, Barcelona in the middle, and Tarragona in the south. To the north, the frontier with France (now, but not in the past) lies along the Pyrenees, and to the east is the Mediterranean. In area Catalonia is about the size of Holland or Belgium. Two mountain spurs extend south from the Pyrenees, one towards Barcelona and the other further and deeper inland, so that apart from a narrow coastal plain the landscape is rugged and broken and has been described as a flight of stairs rising from the coast to the 3400m (11,000 ft) peak of Mount Aneto in the Pyrenees. The existence of passes through the eastern Pyrenees has from the earliest times made Catalonia a corridor between the Iberian Peninsula and the rest of Europe and laid it open to successive incursions, often short-lived as the invaders passed on, from Carthaginians, Romans, Visigoths, Moors, and the Franks to their descendants, the French. This is one reason why the Catalans regard themselves as Europeans as much as Spaniards.

Catalonia is often described as rich in natural resources, but this is not so. It possesses few minerals and only two sizable tracts of arable land: the plains of Empordà at the foot of the Pyrenees and of Urgell east of Lleida. An abundance of fish from the Mediterranean, and the cultivation of vines, fruit and olives, and of rice in the sub-tropical Ebro delta, have nevertheless made Catalonia all but self-sufficient in food.

The traditional wealth of Catalonia has resulted from the industry of its people in processing raw materials brought from outside; an exception has been its wine and spirit trade, with native-produced cork as a valuable ancillary. Barcelona, once known for textiles, is now heavily industrialized and the region as a whole has attracted more than two million workers from poorer parts of Spain.

GETTING AROUND

There are train and bus services between the major towns, but to see anything of the country districts and the scenic mountain regions a car is essential. Most of the main roads radiate

11

from Barcelona and run north and south (with the exception of the N 11 to Lleida). A good touring map, such as the 1 cm : 3 km Firestone sheet or 1 cm : 4 km Michelin map is a necessity; it is well to bear in mind that the enticing cross-country roads in yellow or green, though well-surfaced, are often slow – the scenic interest and the time taken is generally in proportion to the number of zig-zags on the map. By using the *autopistas* (motorways) and national highways (N roads) it is possible to get from almost any point to another in Catalonia within half a day's driving – but be warned: to cross Barcelona or drive in or out of it may well take hours. This applies especially to weekends (beware Friday and Sunday evenings), when there is a mass exodus to and from the country. The *autopistas* are toll roads, but the charges are moderate and well worth the saving in time and stress on cross-country journeys.

LANGUAGE

After the Civil War of 1936–39 the use of Catalan, both as a spoken and written language, was totally banned by the Franco government. Since 1946, when magazines and books could once again be printed in Catalan, and after 1978 when it was reinstated as an official language in Spain, things have turned full circle. It is now a matter of pride to speak in Catalan, and it is taught in all schools. Road signs and place names are usually both in Catalan and Spanish, though teenage chauvinists, in place of graffiti, often demonstrate their independence by scrawling over the Spanish version.

Catalan, like other Romance languages such as Italian or Castilian, had its origins in a fusion of the native tongue with the conversational Latin of the towns and cities founded by the Romans. It is much closer to the *langue d'oc* of southern France – with which Catalonia had close links throughout the medieval period – than to Castilian, much influenced by a massive transfusion of Arabic words. Catalan differs from the other better-known Romance languages in the occurrence of the curious diphthongs, *au*, *eu*, and *iu*, which together with strong syllabic stress and the absence of nasal and silent terminations, gives the spoken language a somewhat harsh and rugged character. Spanish-speaking visitors will find no difficulty, since Castilian is everywhere spoken and understood, and in fact only about half of the population speaks Catalan, though the proportion is rising and Catalan is also spoken in the *paisos catalans*, the territories once ruled by the Kingdom of Aragon (*see* Chapter II) and comprising the provinces of Castellón de la

Plana and Valencia, the Balearic Islands, Andorra and the
Roussillon in France.

With a working knowledge of French and Castilian and the rudiments of school Latin one can make a fist of reading Catalan, though it requires study to enjoy and appreciate the Catalan classics (*see* Chapter III). The larger restaurants and hotels provide versions of the menu in Castilian, English and French (but to help in this direction, the names of popular dishes are given in Catalan and English in Chapter V). In one instance the Catalans make no concessions to visitors: this is on the notices of opening hours outside cathedrals, museums and official buildings. The key words are:

obert	open	*Dinmenge*	Sunday
tancat	closed	*Dilluns*	Monday
dias de feina, dias obrers	weekdays	*Dimarts*	Tuesday
		Dimecres	Wednesday
festes	holidays	*Dijous*	Thursday
		Divendres	Friday
		Dissabte	Saturday

In a book for English-speaking readers, spelling is something of a problem, because many words and names are more familiar in their Castilian version. We have spelt the names of people and places in Catalan wherever applicable, sometimes giving the Castilian form too. Other terms are not specifically Catalan, and we have, for example, used the word '*autopista*', in general use on maps, to describe a motorway (or turnpike in the USA) because the Catalan '*autovia*' would not be understood by most readers.

MEAL TIMES

The Catalans, like the Spaniards generally, eat late. You may as well resign yourself to dining at 9 p.m. or 10 p.m. at the earliest (especially if invited by Catalan friends), and bring with you a pack of cards, travel scrabble or a chunky paperback or two to while away the time.

Breakfast (*azmorzar*) is at the usual hour from 7 a.m. to 10 a.m. The Paradors (*see* p.14) and many hotels now offer a buffet with fruit juices and fruit; cereals; rolls, croissants and pastries; make-it-yourself toast; cheese; cold ham; eggs, boiled or fried; bacon and hot *botifarra* sausage; and the Catalan speciality which goes so well with much of this, *pa amb tomàquet* (*see* p.205). This is more interesting than a continental breakfast brought to one's bedroom, and even the Catalans are beginning to eat a cooked breakfast given half a chance. We were recently breakfasting at the Parador at Arties in the Pyrenees, when there was a sudden flurry of guests. They turned out to have left Barcelona at 6 a.m. to attend a wedding later in the day and to a man (and woman) were soon fortifying themselves with bacon and eggs.

Most shops and offices are closed from 1 p.m. to 4.30 p.m., and the main meal of the day is lunch (*dinar*), which in restaurants and hotels is usually served from 1.30 p.m. to 4 p.m. Most offer a set *menú del dia*, but portions are so substantial it is often better and less expensive to order something lighter *à la carte*.

To bridge the yawning gap until the evening meal, there is *berenar* (*merienda*) from about 5 p.m. to 7 p.m. This might comprise an *entrepá* (a crusty meat-filled roll), or coffee or chocolate with pastries.

Supper (*sopar*) is late, often at about 11 p.m. when eaten at home, and is lighter and more informal than the main meal in the middle of the day, often consisting of soup, a *truita de patata* (*tortilla*: a Spanish potato and onion omelette) and fresh fruit. Restaurants do not normally begin serving dinner until 9 p.m. to 10 p.m., though the Paradors and hotels catering for foreigners take compassion on their guests and start at 8.30 p.m.

There is a list of recommended restaurants on pp.195–8; if you find it difficult to adjust to their hours and want to eat early, the best thing is to head for a *cafeteria*, where light food, such as toasted sandwiches, omelettes and *plats combinats* (mixed dishes), is available at any time.

HOTELS AND PARADORS

Hotels and pensions in Catalonia are currently being reclassified. Hotels are now rated one star to five stars according to their amenities, service and degree of luxury; all must provide private bathrooms in the bedrooms. The old categories of simpler establishments, such as *hostales* and *fondas*, are being discontinued. Instead, there are now, or will shortly be, only one-star and two-star *pensions*, the first containing fifteen per cent of rooms with bath and the others twenty-five per cent.

In Barcelona, where there are conferences and trade fairs from one end of the year to the other, it is always advisable to book as much ahead as possible. During the summer season hotels in holiday places are also very full.

A comprehensive list of hotels, and also of restaurants, may be found in the red *Michelin Guide to Spain and Portugal*. There are also seven Paradors (state-owned hotels) in Catalonia, at Arties, Vielha and La Seu d'Urgell in the Pyrenees; Vic and Cardona in Barcelona Province; Aiguablava on the Costa Brava; and Tortosa in Tarragona Province. Cardona is a historic monument and all are sited in picturesque surroundings. They offer impressive reception rooms, spacious bedrooms and bathrooms, and quiet, relaxing dining rooms serving some regional dishes.

I · The Catalans in their history

It is a heady, but perilous, exercise to generalize about national character; and with Catalonia the task is complicated by successive and massive immigrations of peasants from poorer parts of Spain, notably Murcia and the south, which have swelled the present population by about two million. Nonetheless, the Spaniards are the first to admit that the Catalans do possess very marked characteristics of their own.

Writing in his *Handbook for Travellers in Spain* in 1845, Richard Ford declared with his usual verve:

> No province of the unamalgamated bundle which forms the conventional monarchy of Spain hangs more loosely to the crown than Catalonia, the classical country of revolt, which is ever ready to fly off: rebellious and republicans, well may the natives wear the blood-coloured cap of the much prostituted name of liberty.

There is much truth in this, but Ford touches on another and fundamental aspect of the Catalans, when he further describes them as 'frugal, honest and rough diamonds'. According to the Castilian proverb, 'The Catalans get bread out of stones'; and it has been a capacity for hard work, often in the face of defeat and disaster, which has enabled them to make a country with few natural resources one of the richest regions of Spain. Theirs is a tradition very different from that of Castile and the south, where in the period following the fall of Granada in 1492, the Old Christians tended to leave the manual jobs to Moors living in the reconquered territories and the professions and trade to the Jews, in the belief that such employment was unworthy of a Christian, who was held to be specially fitted for soldiering, priesthood or government. To the Catalan, on the other hand, manual or trading activity was a source of pride; and this resulted in the emergence of a bourgeoisie with no counterpart in Castile; in less differentiation between social classes; and in possibilities for an individual to move from one class to another by dint of his own efforts.

An innate respect for the rights of the individual took tangible shape as early as 1068 in the form of the *usatges*, a code of usage predating Magna Carta by a century and a half (*see* p.22). This was reinforced by the formation in the

thirteenth century of the Corts (or Parliament) with much
greater powers than the Castilian Cortes.

A facet of the Catalan's individuality is that he has always
remained intensely conscious of his ancient rights and privileges. There is a Catalan expression *no hi ha dret*, meaning
that it is not right, or against the agreed law of the land. If Ford
was implying that when the Catalan dons 'the blood-coloured
cap of liberty' he wears it *well*, his comment is perhaps justified
in that, for all their violence, revolutions in Catalonia have been
an outraged reaction to the infringement of traditional or
national liberties. Contradictory as it may sound, the Catalan
has often been a conservative revolutionary; and, whether or
not a long-standing custom was still sensible or applicable in
changed circumstances, he has fought to retain it.

This conservatism manifests itself in other ways; few Catalans holiday in other parts of Spain or abroad, they mostly
spend August in the mountains or on the coast; they dress
soberly, dislike bullfights and are not given to propping up
bars. A long-held tradition among country folk is that the
eldest son of the *masia* (or farm) inherits the whole property
and the younger sets up on his own, and the enterprise of small
manufactories is still to be reckoned with in a world where
multinational business organizations and foreign-inspired
labour movements are undermining traditional concepts of
nationalism.

BEGINNINGS

'If we are a Latin people', wrote the perspicacious Miguel
Tarradell, 'it is because for seven centuries we lived under the
great civilizing influence of the Romans — and not because the
role of nationhood had been assigned to us from the time of
Adam and Eve.' There had been foreign visitations from the
Phoenicians and the Greeks, and more determined inroads by
the Carthaginians — it is said that Hamilcar Barca gave his own
name of Barcino to Barcelona — but the historical watershed was
the landing of Gnaeus Cornelius Scipio at Empúries in 218 BC.

Thereafter, Romanization gathered pace with the establishment of law and order, the development of agriculture and the
construction of a network of properly engineered roads —
portions of the Via Augusta, which crossed the Pyrenees at La
Jonquera and continued through Girona, Barcelona, and then
southwards along the coast, still survive. As a result, the
indigenous population began moving down from defensive
positions in the hills, and cities were created, each a miniature
Rome and perhaps the most potent of the Empire's means of

17

civilization. The largest in the region were Valencia, Barcelona and Tarragona (Tarraco), which became the capital of the province of Tarraconensis, embracing the whole of the north and centre of Roman Hispania.

The wealthy bourgeoisie often owned *villae* with extensive orchards and gardens on the outskirts of the towns, and these were the forerunners of the *mas* or *masia*, so characteristic of Catalonia, many of which remain today. They are strongly built stone houses, well adapted for defence in earlier days, on two floors with a sloping roof. Formerly the ground floor accommodated animals and farm implements as well as the kitchen, the centre of family life. The upper floor housed bedrooms and a large *sala*, used on formal occasions. Some of the larger *masies*, especially in the Empordà, are most imposing, with an arcaded balcony in Romanesque style on the upper floor.

So important was the *masia* that it often gave its name to the family; and the paramount importance of keeping it in the family gave birth to the tradition that the eldest son should inherit the whole estate or that, at best, in accordance with Roman law, any younger children should share the *legitima* or third part of the property.

Mas Rabell de Fontenac, a 14th-century Catalan *masia*

There were two other consequences of the Roman occupation of even more lasting significance than physical remains or
technical advances in agriculture: the spread of Christianity
and the birth of the Catalan language.

Christianity first took root in the cities connected to Rome
by sea or by the Via Augusta. It is difficult to say whether there
is any truth in the legend that St Paul visited Tarragona and
was the country's first evangelist. Certain it is that clandestine
groups of Christians were well established by the middle of the
third century AD, when a bishop and two deacons of Tarragona, Fruitós, Auguri and Eulogi, suffered martyrdom. Somewhat later two missionaries from North Africa were executed;
Sant Feliu at Girona, and Sant Cugat at Barcelona. Notwith-
standing, there was no systematic persecution of Christians –
for the Romans, religion was always more a matter of politics
than metaphysics, and by the early years of the fifth century,
coinciding with the first invasion of the Visigoths, and as in
other parts of the tottering Empire, Christianity had become
the official religion of the country.

Christianity was in the first place an urban religion, but as it
slowly spread into the country districts it was largely the
influence of the Church which influenced people in the more
remote mountain regions to abandon their native tongue in
favour of Vulgar Latin, the forerunner of Catalan. 'Language is
the perfect instrument of empire,' remarked the Bishop of Avila
to Isabel the Catholic, when presenting her with a copy of
Nebrija's Spanish grammar in 1492. At numerous points in
their history the Catalans have fought for their language – after
the union with Castile, after their defeat in the War of the
Spanish Succession and under the regime of General Franco.
Nowadays it is spoken everywhere, and most Catalan his-
torians and novelists, though equally fluent in Castilian – and
difficult as it may be for the world in general to read their books
– prefer to write in their native tongue. What, under the
Romans, started as a unifying influence, has by a full turn of the
wheel become an emblem of national independence.

THE SPANISH MARK

Three centuries of Gothic rule did little to efface the civilizing
influence of the Romans. No part of Hispania was less firmly
attached to the body general than the north-eastern corner, and
when, after their first landing in 711, the Moors swept through
the Peninsula and into France they were first accepted as allies.
It was not long, however, before Barcelona was occupied by the
Moorish governor of al-Andalus and it took twenty years of

hard fighting for the Franks under Charles Martel and later Charlemagne to drive back the invaders across the Pyrenees. By this time the Catalans, as they first became known at this period, had thrown in their hand with the Franks. So, in the words of the *Chronicle* of the Abbey of Moissac:

> The Goths or Spaniards, inhabitants of the famous city of Barcelona, fleeing the cruel yoke of the Saracens, the enemies of Christ, approached us and freely gave or ceded their city to our authority; and removing themselves from the power of the Saracens, they submitted to our rule by free and prompt decision.

In this voluntary submission to the Carolingians was founded the area of northern Spain known as the *Marca hispanica* or Spanish Mark. Charlemagne on his side promised to cooperate in freeing Barcelona and the Moorish-occupied region while promising to respect the rights of their inhabitants – a pledge which was kept. Barcelona was liberated by the Franks in 801, but remained anything but secure and in 813 it was sacked by the Moors. The chronicler Ibn-Hayyan recounts how the severed heads of the defenders were piled into a bloody pyramid, exceeding the height of a lance stuck into the ground, from the top of which a muezzin exhorted the victorious troops.

The Spanish Mark remained a distant province of the Carolingian Empire, and its detachment came about not as the result of a violent rebellion or upsurge of nationalistic feeling, but more by default. While the power of the sovereign decreased, that of his vassals, the counts, steadily grew, so that in the final resort it was no longer the king who chose the counts, but the counts who chose the king, and the Empire began to split into independent principalities.

In Catalonia there was a tendency for the Count of Barcelona to take precedence over his fellows, and the founder of the House of Barcelona, which was to rule the country for the next five centuries, was Guifré el Pilós (Wilfred the Hairy). Legend has it that while fighting against the Moors with Charles the Bald, he was wounded. The king thereupon dipped his fingers into the blood and drew them across Wilfred's gilded shield, so making a grant of arms and originating the Catalan flag with its red bars on a yellow ground.

By the time of his death in 897 at the hands of the Moorish governor of Lleida, Wilfred had succeeded in resettling the regions devastated by the Moors and in uniting under his rule most of the counties of Catalonia. For another century the Catalan nobility paid lip service to the edicts of the Carolingians, but Count Ramon Borrell of Barcelona initiated a policy openly hostile to the Franks. In the face of a last and savage Moorish onslaught in 985 under the all-conquering al-Mansur, Borrell pocketed his pride and applied to Lothaire, King of the Franks for help, but met with a dusty answer. Borrell sat it out in the mountains; the Moors retired some six months later; and the Counts, breaking off all relations with the Franks, now became sovereigns in their own land.

Guifré el Pilós (Wilfred
the Hairy), founder of
the House of Barcelona

THE HOUSE OF BARCELONA

The death of al-Mansur in 1002 and the disintegration of the Cordoban Caliphate was a turning point in the history of the Iberian Peninsula. Henceforth, in a reversal of roles, it was the Christians of the north who were to harry and demand tribute from the Moors. In Catalonia, Ramon Berenguer I (1035–76) had so extended his territories and consolidated his position that he felt strong enough to introduce a historic declaration of rights. The *usatges*, which begin by stating that 'without truth and justice the iniquitous prince destroys himself together with his lands and their inhabitants', constitute a written code defining the rights and responsibilities of the ruler on the one

21

hand, and of his subjects on the other. If, as in the case of Magna Carta, a study of their contents suggests that their compilers were less interested in the rights of the common people and more concerned with preserving their own, they nevertheless mark a great step forward in that the rights of the individual were for the first time defined.

It has been said that the reign of Ramon Berenguer III (1096–1131) 'opened windows on Europe'. By now the northern counties of Besalú, Cerdanya, Pellars, Empúries and also Roussillon and Foix were all firmly under the control of the Counts of Barcelona. Outwitting the formidable Alfons I d'Aragó (el Bataller), Ramon Berenguer, in a manoeuvre that was to become the hallmark of the Counts of Barcelona, married the fair Dolça, heiress to Provence, so gaining possession of her territories. The alliance was to last for more than a century and a half and led both countries to an expansion of sea-borne trade and, through a shared language and the poetry of the Provençal troubadours, to the cultural awakening of Catalonia.

Relations between Catalonia and her powerful neighbours to the west and south, Aragon and Castile, were alike strained. There had been fighting between Aragonese and Catalan troops over the possession of Lleida, and the imperialistic ambitions of Castile were undisguised. Ramon Berenguer IV (1131–62) was vividly aware of the danger of a union between the two. In the event, on the death of Alfons el Bataller, his son Ramir retired to a monastery, and possession of Aragon hung on the marriage of his two year-old daughter, Perenella. Ramon Berenguer, forestalling a similar move from Castile, moved smartly in and secured Perenella's hand and kingdom. Under the terms of the marriage settlement, Perenella retained the title of Queen of Aragon and Ramon Berenguer was to be known as *Princeps Aragonum*. Only after his death would his descendants take the title of 'King of Aragon and Count of Barcelona'. His modesty has been put down to a desire to avoid offending the Aragonese nobility, but it also sprang from natural pride. 'I,' said the Count, according to the *Chronicle* of Bernat Desclot, 'received the lady with no wish to be called king; I am now one of the premier counts of the world, and if I were to be called king, I should not be one of the greatest.' Although Catalonia was henceforth to be the dominant force, the combined realm was known as the *Corona d'Aragó* (Crown of Aragon).

Jaume I (James the Conqueror, 1213–76), whose father was killed and lost most of the Catalan territories beyond the Pyrenees to Simon de Montfort in the disastrous battle of

Muret in 1213, was only nine when he succeeded to the
throne. His military exploits included the capture of Mallorca
from the Moors in 1229 and of Valencia in 1238. Of even more
significance in the long run were his policies for repopulating
the reconquered territories and ensuring an adequate labour
force on the land. Unlike their Castilian counterparts, the
nobility received no vast estates and the main beneficiaries
were the Catalan knights. By this means, instead of fostering a
powerful and rebellious aristocracy, he laid the foundations for
a farming and mercantile class which would rally to the crown
in hour of need.

Sometimes criticized as an unlettered barbarian, Jaume made
Catalan the official language of the country and was responsible for the first of the four great Catalan chronicles, the *Llibre
dels Feits*, heralding the literary achievements of the following
decades.

QUEEN OF THE MEDITERRANEAN

With the conquest of Valencia, Catalonia could expand no
further inside Spain and was now set to play a larger role on the

Jaume I (James the
Conqueror), from
Ramon Llull's *Aureum
opus*, 1515

23

European stage. Repeating the tactic of his forbears, Jaume had in 1260 married his eldest son Pere (Peter), the future Pere I ('The Great'), to Constança, daughter of King Manfred of Sicily – a step which aroused the bitter opposition of the two major powers of the time, the Papacy and France. The French force of Charles of Anjou subsequently occupied the island, but in 1282 Pere, who 'happened' to be cruising in the neighbourhood with an army of 15,000 men and 140 ships, took advantage of the outbreak of the rebellion known as the Sicilian Vespers to recover the island in the name of his wife.

So began a twenty-year period during which the Catalans and their famous admiral, Roger de Llúria, trounced the French in the Mediterranean and resisted all attempts to recover the island. The historian Ferrán Soldevila goes to the heart of the matter when he writes:

> Could a nation of mariners, sailors and merchants with the degree of maritime power they had now developed, lose an opportunity such as that afforded by the occupation of Sicily, a base of the first importance in the central Mediterranean, a stepping stone to the Levant and close to the markets of North Africa?

The repercussions were personal and furious. The Pope excommunicated Pere II and conferred his kingdom on Charles of Valois; and the French mounted a crusade against him with a huge army of 16,000 knights, 17,000 crossbowmen and 100,000 infantry, backed up by 100 ships. Surging across the Pyrenees, it was held up by the courageous defence of Girona and the invasion was brought to an ignominious end when Roger de Llúria destroyed the French fleet in the Gulf of Roses in 1285.

Among the most formidable of the soldiers and sailors who beat off the French attacks on Sicily was the freebooting Roger de Flor. At the end of hostilities, he and his troops, the savage Catalan and Aragonese mercenaries, the so-called Almogàvers became a thorn in the flesh of Pere II's son, King Frederic. He was therefore glad to see the back of them when Roger proposed to the Byzantine emperor, Andronicus II, that they should proceed to Constantinople to take part in the struggle against the Ottoman Turks.

The subsequent adventures of the Grand Company of Almogàvers, which arrived in Constantinople in September 1303, have passed into legend. Having massacred the Turks they soon began treating the Greeks whom they had been sent to liberate like conquered enemies. Roger de Flor was ambushed and murdered by the Emperor's son, Michael, but the Grand Company soldiered on under new commanders and became masters of the Duchy of Athens, which was made over to King Frederic and remained under Sicilian control until 1387.

The Catalan-Aragonese empire in the Mediterranean was extended during the reign of Pere III; and after the last representative of the House of Barcelona, Martí el Jove (Martin the Young) died suddenly in 1409 while on an expedition to Sardinia, Alfons V ('The Magnanimous', 1416–58) spent his life campaigning for the Kingdom of Naples. This he finally won in 1442, but only at the expense of aggravating Catalonia's many internal problems by his constant demands for money.

These problems stemmed from much earlier in the fourteenth century when the Crown of Aragon was to all appearances at the zenith of its powers, with its far-flung consulates, its merchants engaged in the Alexandria spice trade, and its sailors ranging the Mediterranean and Atlantic alike. They began with the Black Death and the collapse of the banking system, but at the heart of the country's ills was the bitter and growing dispute between the *pagesos de remença*, the peasants tied to the land, and the landed proprietors. In the main, some ninety per cent of the ruling hierarchy and the Corts and Generalitat which represented them were ranged against the *pagesos*, while the Crown took their side. A savage dog-fight developed, lasting for ten years and embroiling Louis XI of France on the side of the king, Joan (John) II. The only true loser was Catalonia itself, which after all the blood-letting and disruption of war was deprived of the counties of Roussillon and Cerdanya, seized by Louis XI, and left in a position of demographic and economic inferiority to Castile.

UNION WITH CASTILE

At the centre of the arcaded Plaça Reial in Barcelona, where the *tertulias* sit late into the night over their glasses of beer, there once stood a plinth destined for an equestrian statue of Ferran II el Catòlic (Ferdinand the Catholic). It was demolished in 1869 by order of the City Council, no doubt because the Catalan writers of the *Renaixença*, the romantic and nationalistic movement of the nineteenth century, laid at his feet the lion's share of the blame for the depressed and decadent state of the Principality during the sixteenth century.

Ferdinand, son of King Joan II, had married Isabel of Castile as a political move to enlist Castilian help in ending the civil war, but Isabel remained ruler of Castile, and Ferdinand

Catalonia

Ferran II (el Catòlic) of
Aragon and Isabel I of
Castile, *Los Reyes
Catolicos*

Woodcut from the *Llibre
de cosolat*, 1552, an
historic book on
maritime law

Catalan merchants, from
the *Consulado del Mar*,
1539

retained the Crown of Aragon. By forcing the Inquisition on a country rootedly opposed to it, Ferdinand did Catalonia a disservice; it has been estimated that just over three per cent of the population of Barcelona was affected. In other directions he did much to contribute to the recuperation of Catalonia, agreeing with the Corts (Parliament) in 1481 that any royal measure in breach of the laws and usages of Catalonia be declared null and void; securing a fair settlement for the *pagesos* which led to a revival of the rural economy; and stimulating basic industries by granting monopolies for the export of cloth and taking energetic measures to stamp out the piracy rampant in the Mediterranean.

If Ferdinand can hardly be accused of the 'Castilianization' of government, matters took a different turn with the accession of

his grandson, the Holy Roman Emperor Charles V (Charles I of Spain). Even though he and his Habsburg successors continued to style themselves, not 'King of Spain' but 'King of the Spains', the kingship was now combined in one person and centred on Madrid. The Crown of Aragon was now only a small unit of an Empire reaching out to the Low Countries, Germany, Italy and the New World. Deprived of her former proud role of mistress of the Mediterranean, Catalonia became increasingly inward-looking and turned a deaf ear to pleas for help from Valencia and Aragon in the face of centralist incursion – thus going a long way to sever the remaining links between the partners in the Crown of Aragon.

By the beginning of the seventeenth century, a gulf had opened between Catalonia and the Madrid government. It was argued in Madrid that the Crown of Aragon should play its share in shouldering the burden of Empire; the Catalans took the view that the religious and dynastic wars in Europe were not of the Principality's seeking and that Catalonia had been denied fair participation in the great venture in the Indies. When the chief minister of Philip IV, the formidable Count Duke of Olivares, overruled Catalan laws forbidding the raising of troops for foreign service – 'If the constitutions do not allow this, then *the devil take the constitutions* and whoever observes them' – and further billeted 9000 of his own troops on the Principality, the Corts were forthwith summoned by trumpet and the Council of One Hundred by ringing of the city bell. But it was now too late to avoid an explosion. In June 1640 a mob of 500 *segadors* (harvesters) burst into Barcelona, attempted to set fire to the palace of the viceroy, the Count of Santa Coloma, and murdered him as he tried to board a Genoese galley.

Philip V, the first of the Spanish Bourbons, began his reign with a prompt visit to Barcelona in 1701 and by granting the Corts concessions which, in the words of his secretary, made them 'more independent of him than the Parliament of England'. It was not enough, and in the ensuing War of the Spanish Succession the Catalans decided to throw in their lot with the Archduke Charles of Austria and the Grand Alliance of England, Austria and Holland. Unfortunately the Allies were less than scrupulous in implementing their guarantees, and Barcelona was left to defend itself against Philip's army of 20,000 reinforced by the French under the Duke of Berwick.

With conspicuous gallantry the Catalans held out for fourteen months, but, as Jaime Vicens Vives has written, in attempting to maintain their regional laws and the pluralistic concept of the Spanish Monarchy, they 'were fighting against the current of history and the price for this is usually very high.'

Harvesters storming the viceroy's palace in Barcelona on 7 June 1640

So it was to prove. Under the *Decreto de Nueva Planta* of 1716, the Council of One Hundred and the Generalitat were abolished; books were collected and destroyed; Barcelona University was transferred to the small provincial town of Cervera; and a Captain General was appointed, together with a high court or *Audiencia*, in which all proceedings were to be conducted in Castilian.

PHOENIX FROM THE ASHES

If 19 January 1716 remains one of the blackest days in Catalan history and the *Nueva Planta* imposed an artificial political unity out of key with deeply-held feelings and beliefs, it nevertheless opened up domestic and foreign markets, channelling Catalan energies into industry and commerce. Economic revival began in agriculture, especially in the production of wine in the Penedès and the export of brandy to an expanding market in England; and the profits were ploughed back into a new industry for the manufacture of cotton cloth. During the period of 'enlightened despotism', Charles III (1759–88) and his ministers swept away Cadiz's American monopoly, allowing other ports in Spain, including Barcelona and Tarragona, to trade directly with Cuba and South America. As a result, exports from Barcelona increased ten times in a single decade.

Such was the vitality of the region that within a century the population had doubled to almost a million, and it was in fact about 1780 that the image of the hard-working, pushful Catalan businessman first became current in Madrid. By this time the intense economic activity in the coastal region was bringing about profound changes in Catalan society. In the mountainous hinterland life continued largely along feudal lines, with the landed proprietors and clergy securely entrenched. In Barcelona the great cotton boom gave birth to a new middle-class bourgeoisie, and at the same time the new factories created a demand for labour, met by an influx of workers from country districts as far afield as Andalucia. Unrest among the manual workers found violent expression in the *rebomboris de pa* or bread riots of 1789, which set a pattern for the militant workers' movements of the nineteenth century.

Industrial development was interrupted during the earlier part of the century by two extended wars. After Napoleon had launched the Peninsula War (known in Spain as *La Guerra de la Independencia*), Barcelona was one of the first cities to fall, in February 1808. Crossing the southern end of the Pyrenees with 14,000 men, General Duhesme advanced unopposed, and the city was treacherously occupied when General Lecchi marched a column of troops past the fortress, apparently on his way out, then gave sudden orders to wheel and occupy it. Girona was not to succumb to such tactics. After the French had been beaten off in August 1808 and harried from the sea by a British naval detachment under the Lord Cochrane, the siege was resumed in May 1809 and has gone down as the most heroic engagement of the whole campaign. A series of sorties on the part of the Spanish commander, Mariano Alvarez de Castro, inflicted disastrous losses on the French, and it was only in December 1809, with Alvarez ill and delirious, that the starving garrison, who had cost the French the best part of a year's campaigning season, finally surrendered.

The struggle against the French in Catalonia was most

Lord Cochrane, who
routed the Napoleonic
forces at Roses

effectively conducted by the armed peasantry, the so-called
miqueletes and *sometents*, but there was little or nothing to
show for their homeric sacrifices. When the last battle of the
war was fought at Molins del Rei in Catalonia on 10 January
1814, agriculture was at a low ebb, imports of grain had been
disrupted by the British naval blockade and the famine of 1812
was followed by epidemics in which people died in thousands.

Before his death in September 1833, the restored Ferdinand
VII of Spain remarked that 'Spain is a bottle of beer and I am
the cork. Without me it would all go off in froth.' He was
proved speedily right; civil war broke out only a few days after
his funeral, between the supporters of his wife, Queen Christ-
ina and her daughter Isabella, and his brother, Don Carlos. The
war was more than a dynastic struggle: Don Carlos was a

devout and convinced Catholic, who fiercely resented the erosion of the Church's political influence and drew most of his support in Catalonia from the 'absolutists'. Their primary object was to maintain their own institutions against encroachment from Madrid, while Barcelona and the coastal area were overwhelmingly liberal and pledged their support to the Queen.

The war was fought with the utmost ferocity and ended in 1840 with victory for the liberals, when General Espartero captured the Carlist headquarters at Morella. Although the war between absolutists and liberals was to break out on two further occasions during the nineteenth century, in Catalonia politics were henceforth to be dominated by two main issues: the struggle of the manual workers for better conditions, and the campaign for regional autonomy mounted by the bourgeoisie and middle classes.

RENAISSANCE

The labour movement took definite shape in 1830 with the organization of trade unions (*societats de resistencia al capital*) by the textile workers in Barcelona. In 1838 a Liberal government reluctantly recognized the right of assembly for mutual aid, which was to lead to the formation of co-operatives, workers' atheneums, choirs and cultural centres, so typical of the labour tradition in Catalonia. After violent protests about the installation of automatic machinery, and the burning of factories, a ban on labour unions resulted in a general strike in Barcelona in July 1855. This was a curtain raiser to the perennial labour troubles and terrorism for which Barcelona was to become a byword.

From the start the Catalan labour movement was Anarchist-inspired – the natural result of a political system in which the right to vote was linked with the payment of property tax. Its prime concern was with the betterment of working conditions, but during the latter decades of the nineteenth century, social struggles grew increasingly violent. In revenge for repressive measures or the execution of their comrades, there were attacks on King Alfonso XII and his successor, Alfonso XIII; two prime ministers, Antonio Canovas and Eduardo Dato, were assassinated; and 1909 saw an unprecedented outbreak of violence, the so-called 'Tragic Week', in which workers set fire to churches and convents from one end of Barcelona to another in protest against the mobilization of reservists for the unpopular colonial war in Morocco. What was to become by far the largest union in the country, the Anarcho-syndicalist CNT, was first formed

Insignia of the Unió Catalanista, one of the first organizations to promote Catalan autonomy

in 1911. Although it numbered a terrorist minority, its leadership was dedicated to the improvement of living conditions, but without direct participation in politics or the recovery of separate nationality for Catalonia.

Like the manual workers, the Catalan manufacturers formed bodies to further their own interests, principally to combat the demands of their employees and to obtain protective tariffs. Linked with the demand for protectionism was the increasing preoccupation of the ebullient bourgeoisie and middle class with regional autonomy. In the first place this started with a literary movement, the so-called *Renaixença* or Renaissance (*see also* Chapter II). In their darkest days Catalans had never lost sight of their identity as a people apart; but since the coming of the Bourbons, the Catalan language, though spoken colloquially, had not been taught in schools or used officially, nor was it considered a suitable medium for literature. By reviving interest in Catalonia's historic past and specifically in the language, the *Renaixença* stimulated attempts to obtain a political structure appropriate to an individual national entity.

By 1892 various Catalanist organizations had banded together as the *Unió Catalanista* and put forward a programme for Catalan autonomy, and in the face of the economic, social and political disruption following the loss of Cuba and the war with the United States, the *Lliga Catalanista* took up the fight. In 1914, under the forceful Fransesc Cambó, it succeeded in wringing a concession from Madrid for the setting up of a Catalan *Mancomunitat* with powers to improve roads, railways and telephones, and to support schools and universities. This was speedily suppressed under the military dictatorship of Primo de Rivera, but in the elections which followed his dismissal in 1930 the *Esquerra republicana de Catalunya* (Catalan Republican Left) won a huge majority. On 14 April 1931, its leader, the charismatic Fransesc Macià, with his white hair, luminous eyes and aristocratic bearing, appeared on the balcony of the historic building of the Generalitat and proclaimed a Catalan Republic as 'an integral part of the Iberian Federation'. In deference to feelings in Madrid, Macià agreed that the new entity should be called the 'Government of the Generalitat', and the Cortes somewhat restricted its functions, nevertheless leaving it with widespread powers.

When Fransesc Macià died on Christmas Day 1933 he was succeeded as President of the Generalitat by Lluis Companys, left of him politically and a former lawyer for the CNT. Companys was still in office when the Civil War broke out in 1936 and was arrested in France during the Nazi occupation and handed over to the Franquist authorities. Before he was

shot on Montjuïc, not half a kilometre from the new Olympic
stadium, he made one last request – that he be allowed to
remove his shoes, so that he might die with his feet touching
Catalan soil.

Barcelona was the last government stronghold to be overrun
by Franco's forces, on 26 January 1939. A mass exodus had
begun on 24 January, and the roads to France were jammed
with refugees, with bombs and driving rain to add to their
misery. By 10 February some 10,000 wounded, 170,000
women and children, 60,000 male civilians and 150,000 men
of the Republican army had crossed the frontier. Franco's
revenge was prompt and vindictive. All unions were dissolved,
the Generalitat disappeared and all laws passed by the Catalan
parliament were annulled. And yet again the use of any
language except Castilian was proscribed. This applied not
only to schools and universities, but even to telephone con-
versations – and telephone boxes bore notices to this effect.

During its latter years the Franquist regime began to relax
the harshest measures. In 1945 only two books were printed in
Catalan; by 1968 the number had risen to 500; but thorough-
going liberalization did not take place until after the death of the
Caudillo. It began in April 1977 with the legalization of the
unions and opposition parties. Meanwhile the Spanish government was negotiating with Josep Tarradellas, President of the
Generalitat in exile, and later that year the Generalitat was
re-established by royal decree with Tarradellas at its head.

Largely as a result of pressure from Catalonia and the Basque
country, Spain is now divided into seventeen autonomous
regions. This does not go as far as dedicated Catalanists would
wish, since key areas such as public finance, energy and
transport remain under the control of the central government;
but perhaps the courageous Abbot of Montserrat, Aureli Maria
Escarré, exiled in 1967 for sheltering opponents of the regime,
spoke both as a Catalan and a Spaniard:

> The great majority of Catalans are not separatists. We have a right,
> like any other minority, to our customs, which have their own
> proper place within Spain. We are Spaniards, but not Castilians.

II · Culture and tradition

THE ROMANESQUE TRADITION

Because Romanesque architecture took root in Catalonia when the Counts of Barcelona cut loose from the Carolingian empire and forged an independent principality, it has perhaps been the single most important influence on the arts in Catalonia. For example, Joan Miró, among the masters of modern Catalan painting, is reputed to have said that the Romanesque tradition coursed through his veins like blood; and he certainly used paint in the flat, decorative manner of a Romanesque wall painting.

Romanesque is the style of architecture that evolved after the collapse of the Roman Empire in the countries of Europe where the Roman Catholic rather than the Orthodox Church prevailed. It lasted until the introduction of the Gothic style about 1200 and is known in Britain as 'Norman'. Romanesque architects adopted various features from the Romans: the semi-circular arch, the round barrel vault and even a modified Corinthian column with a capital of acanthus leaves. They made important advances upon Roman methods by balancing the thrust of heavy vaults and domes with buttresses, and in replacing the massive vaults used by the Romans with a thinner structure supported on curved stone ribs.

The architectural work of the period consists almost entirely of parish churches, monasteries, cathedrals and castles; very few domestic buildings have survived. Catalonia possesses no fewer than 1,900 Romanesque churches and some 200 castles or fortified houses. Early Romanesque churches usually followed the simple plan of a basilica, with aisles and an apse; as the style developed, bell towers or campanili were often added. Churches were built in the wake of the reconquest of the country from the Moors, so that some of the earliest and most satisfactory examples are to be found in the security of the mountains, such as those in the Vall d'Aran with their grey slate steeples.

Of larger-scale buildings one of the loveliest is the ruined Benedictine monastery of Sant Pere de Rodes on a hillside overlooking the azure sea off Cap de Creus. With its crenelated walls and towers, and three-naved church and noble campanile, it is, in the words of the Catalan poet Verdaguer, 'a triumphal arch of Christianity'. Consecrated in 1022, it is a monument to the energies of Oliba, Abbot of Ripoll and later Bishop of Vic, statesman of the Church, who was responsible for so much of the religious architecture of the region. The monastery of Ripoll itself, sometimes called 'the cradle of the race', has been many times destroyed and rebuilt – early in its history by Guifré el Pilós, founder of the House of Barcelona, who is buried there. It has been faithfully reconstructed, but nothing now remains of the original except for the elaborately carved portico. Oliba was equally at home in the fields of diplomacy and learning and founded a library of mathematics, astronomy, poetry and music at Ripoll, and the monastery played a part in transmitting Arabic knowledge to Western Europe – though from 1125 onwards this was overshadowed by the outstanding work of the Toledan school of translators.

CHRONICLERS AND SCIENTISTS

The first expression of Catalan literature was troubadour poetry, which flourished from the middle of the twelfth to the end of the thirteenth century and was more than an extension of the Provençal. Such famous poets as Guillem de Bergada, Ramon Vidal de Besalú, Alfons I and Pere II used a profusion of Catalan words and expressions. If Jaume I, by insisting on the use of Catalan and by the example of his chronicle, the *Llibre dels Feits*, may be called the father of Catalan literature, it was Ramon Llull (1232–1315) who ushered in its Golden Age.

Llull came of an aristocratic Mallorcan family and spent a dissolute youth at court, until, as the story goes, his mistress showed him a terrible cancer affecting her breast, after which he devoted himself to religion and philosophy. During his studies and missionary activities, he ranged Europe and the Middle East and was stoned to death, when over eighty, on a crusade to Bougie in North Africa. Such was his mastery of Catalan prose that it has been said that he did for Catalan what Dante did for Italian. Apart from his famous romance *Blanquerna*, partly autobiographical and written more than a century before Chaucer's *Canterbury Tales*, his books are mainly mystical and philosophical, like the *Llibre d'Amic e Amat*, the *Llibre de contemplació* and the *Llibre de meravelles*.

He also wrote scientific works and was credited by contemporary commentators with some thousand on alchemy alone! Modern scholars have, not unnaturally, come to the conclusion that most, if not all, of the alchemical texts with which he is credited are spurious. Llull nevertheless made solid contribu-

The martyrdom of
Ramon Llull at Bujia in
North Africa, from
Ramon Llull *Ars
inventiva veritatis*, 1515
(an edition published
two centuries after his
death)

tions to science by the thoroughly modern method of direct
observation and had realized long before Columbus that the
earth was spherical, a conclusion he reached in his *Llibre de
contemplació*.

> When my thought imagines the surface of the earth opposite to the
> one we are on, it appears to my intelligence and reason that all the
> stones and water which are on the surface should fall into the
> vacuum. But to those who dwell on that surface of the earth which
> lies opposite to ours, it will appear to the contrary, for they will
> think that we, together with the stones and water on our side, must
> go up, because 'up' will appear to them as 'down', because their
> feet will be placed in a direction opposite to ours.

In the same book he describes the use of the magnetic
needle, well in advance of its mention by the Italian Flavio Gioa
in 1302; and his account of charts and astrolabes for naviga-
tional purposes in the *Arte de Navegar* is evidence of the
proficiency of Catalan seamen. The book remained unbettered
even at the time of Columbus.

Llull made an acute observation as to the rise and fall of the tides, which he put down to 'the fact that the earth being spherical, the water of the sea equally takes the shape of an arc' and that 'the arc formed by the waters must have an opposite basis on which it finds the support without which they could not be maintained'. Carrying the argument a step further, he concluded that there must be land on the far side of the Atlantic, 'a Continent against which the water strikes when displaced, as happens on our side, which is, with respect to the other, the eastern one.'

Another formidable scientific figure was Llull's contemporary Arnold (Arnau) de Vilanova (*c.*1240–1311), also an alchemist of repute, who studied at Montpellier University and was in fact one of the most remarkable figures of medieval medicine, being the first modern exponent of the Hippocratic method of keeping careful case histories. He is best known for his use of alcohol in sterilizing wounds (although he did not, as is sometimes mistakenly said, discover alcohol). His *Regimen Sanitatis ad Inclitum Regem Aragonum*, composed for Jaume II, was the first medieval book to be written on public hygiene and stresses the importance of fresh air, baths and physical exercise and the value of a balanced diet.

At a time when Pope Boniface VIII was the most implacable opponent of Catalan expansion in the Mediterranean, Arnold of Vilanova visited Rome and was at once imprisoned. However, the Pope was suffering agonies from stones in the bladder; Arnold was called in and by designing a special truss and other means succeeded in relieving the condition. The grateful Pope said of him, 'At last I have found a Catalan who does good,' and it seems that because of their subsequent friendship Boniface changed his policy towards the Catalans and signed a peace treaty with Frederic of Sicily.

Jaume I's *Llibre dels Feits* was the first of the four great Catalan *Chronicles* (the others were those of Ramon Muntaner, Bernat Desclot and Peter (Pere) the Ceremonious), of which it has been said that they will 'collectively bear comparison with Villehardouin, Joinville, Froissart or any similar company of contemporary historiographers in Western Europe'. Their graphic and factual style derives from the fact that their authors either took part in the events which they record or consulted eye-witnesses; and two of them were kings who were free to write as bluntly as they chose. Taken together, the *Chronicles* cover a period of about two hundred years. That of Bernat Desclot, written in the clear-cut manner of Xenophon's *Anabasis*, overlaps the *Llibre dels Feits*, and the narrative is then taken up by Muntaner (who sometimes suppresses events discreditable to his patron, James II of Mallorca — but if he does not always tell the whole truth, he nevertheless does not invent, and continued in the *Chronicle* known as that of Peter III but actually written, under strict control of the King, by Bernat Descoll and other collaborators.

'THE LOVELIEST CATALAN'

During the classical age of Catalan literature, roughly corresponding to the fifteenth century, the *pus bell catalesc* ('the loveliest Catalan'), in Muntaner's phrase, echoed down the Mediterranean coast and throughout its shores and islands. The purest model of Catalan prose, later enriched by Italian and Latin words and turns of expression, was perhaps the great *Lo Somni* ('The Dream') by Bernat Metge (1350–1410). Outstanding works of fiction were *Tirant lo Blanc* by Joanot Martorell, a chivalrous romance much praised by Cervantes in *Don Quixote*, and the anonymous *Curial e Guelfa*.

Because of the dominance of the Provençal lyric, prose was more written than poetry and preceded it in the development of Catalan literature. Nevertheless, Catalonia gave birth to some notable poets during the fifteenth century. Among the best were the Valencian Jaume Roig (d.1479), whose *Llibre de les dones* was a satire on women written in four-syllable metre, and Auziàs March (1397–1459), the author of numerous subtle love poems and also religious and moral verse. Poetry received a stimulus through the establishment of the *Jocs florals* ('Floral Games') in Barcelona in 1393, of which Enrique de Villena has left a vivid account in his *Arte de Trober*:

> On the appointed day the mantenedors [judges] and the troubadours assembled in the royal palace where I was staying, whence we proceeded in order ... The floor was carpeted, and the troubadours sat upon two rows of seats in a semicircle, while upon a platform in the middle, as high as an altar and covered with cloth of gold, lay the books of art and the prizes. To the right of this was a seat for the king, who often attended ... Each poet then rose and read in a clear voice his composition, which was written on Damascus paper in different colours in gold and silver letters ... After this, we returned in procession to the palace, the prize winner walking between the mantenedors, while a page, accompanied by minstrels and trumpeters, carried the prize before him. Sweets and wines were then served in the palace ...

Although St Vicens Ferrer (1355–1419) wrote some miracle plays, Catalonia produced no drama of note; but many historical and political works were written, and also translations of the Bible and of important Latin and Italian writers, which were thus introduced to the Peninsula for the first time.

Title page of Jaume
Roig's *Llibre de les dones*
('Book of the Ladies'),
1493

After the union of the Crowns of Aragon and Castile in
1479, Catalan fell out of fashion as a literary medium and was
to be revived only as a result of the *Renaixença* of the
nineteenth century – but not before Joan Lluís Vives had given
expression to all that was best and most typical of Catalan
thought.

Vives, related on his mother's side to Auziàs March, was a
man of the Renaissance. Born in Valencia in 1491, he was
educated at Paris University and spent most of his life in
Bruges, where he became a friend of Erasmus. His quality is
best illustrated by excerpts from his writing:

On the Inquisition, from *De Concordia et Discordia in Humano Genere* (1529):

> Today the clergy too has its jurisdiction, procedure, method of accusation; its witnesses, judges, police; its prisons, hangmen, sword, fire, poison ... And in the hands of this clergy is the priesthood of that same Christ who, being the judge of the quick and the dead, yet answered one who wanted Him to advise his brother to divide their heritage: 'Who has made me to judge between you?'

From *De Tradendis Disciplinis* (1531):

> Princes, are for the most part, so corrupt of heart and so intoxicated by the magnitude of their good fortune that by no skill can they be reformed for the better, since they show themselves harsh and unperceptive to those who would cure them ...

And again from his *Subventione Pauperum* (1526), perhaps the most eloquent and moving of his books, in which he sets out his views on sociology and the dignity of man, arguing that the care of the sick, the needy, the blind and the mentally disturbed is a public duty:

> The causes of poverty are wars with the ensuing economic distress; continuous increase of population; a wrong basis in our economic system; and above all, insufficient education ...

THE RENAIXENÇA

Catalan had to all intents and purposes disappeared as a literary vehicle when in 1815 Josep Pau Ballot, an elderly priest and professor of rhetoric, published his *La Gramàtica i apologia de la llengua catalana*, which was at once a dictionary and eulogy of the language. It was the first step towards the *Renaixença*, a romantic movement along the lines of those started in Provence by the poet Mistral and in England by the Pre-Raphaelites, which sought to revive the heritage of the past. The movement is generally held to date from the publication in 1833 of the poem *La pàtria* by Bonaventura Carles Aribau. Curiously enough, it was composed simply as one of various birthday tributes, in several languages, to the Madrid banker, Gaspar de Remisa; but it was the first poem of any importance to have been written in Catalan for almost three centuries, and its nostalgic feeling for country and language caused other poets, including Joaquim Rubio i Ors, to follow Aribau's example. The reinstatement of the *Jocs Florals* (*see* p.38) in 1859 stimulated other writers to use their native language, including the twenty-year-old Jacint Verdaguer (1845–1902), who took the proceedings by storm when he appeared at the prize-giving ceremony dressed as a peasant in the traditional sock-shaped red woollen hat.

Together with the playwright Angel Guimera, Verdaguer was to become the leading protagonist of the *Renaixença*. The son of a quarry worker, he entered the priesthood and became chaplain to the millionaire Marquis of Comillas in Barcelona. Here his fame grew with the publication of his epic poems *L'Atlàntida*, later set to music by Manuel de Falla, and the remarkable *Canigó*. Some 100,000 copies of his *Oda a Barcelona* were distributed to the city's schoolchildren, but at the height of his popularity his championing of the underdog and an altercation with the Bishop of Vic led to his being defrocked. It was a humiliation which divided Barcelona society, but from which he never fully recovered, and he died in poverty.

Catalan was given definitive vocabulary and style with the publication by Pompeu Fabra of his dictionary, as important to present-day Catalans as Dr Johnson's in eighteenth-century England. Fabra founded the Institute of Catalan Studies in 1907 and was involved in the emerging Modernist movement.

MODERNISM AND GAUDÍ

Language is the most potent assertion of national individuality – witness the similar revival of Welsh or Basque – and it was only logical that the *Renaixença* should lead to Catalanism on the political front and to Modernism (*Modernisme*), which looked forward rather than to the past, among architects and artists.

At the turn of the century Barcelona, with its upsurge in industry and a burgeoning entrepreneurial class with an appetite not only for consumer goods but for architecture, music and the arts, was in a state of intellectual and creative ferment. A trio of architects rode the crest of the wave. Luis Domènech i Montaner (1850–1923) exactly caught the spirit of the era in his Palau de la Música Catalana, with its soaring masses of decorative sculpture, its ceramics and stained glass ceiling, inaugurated in 1908 as a home for the Orféo Català, the famous choir. Josep Puig i Cadafalch (1867–1957), professor and politician as well as architect, designed buildings both in neo-Gothic and *modernista* style. Most famous of all was Antoni Gaudí (1852–1926), a figure of world stature and probably one of the most significant architects of his time.

Some of the best work of all three – Domenech's Casa Lleo Morera, Puig's Casa Amatller and Gaudí's Casa Batlló – can conveniently be seen and compared in the Passeig de Gracia, in Barcelona's fashionable shopping area, where the buildings stand almost side by side.

Antoni Gaudí was born in Reus near Tarragona, the son, the grandson and the great grandson of coppersmiths, and maintained that it was at his father's forge that he first developed his feeling for decoration and space. As he later pointed out, 'the coppersmith must fashion a volume from a plate. Before starting out the coppersmith has to see the whole space ... [he] embraces all three dimensions and thus unconsciously has a command of space that not every man possesses.' At seventeen Gaudí entered the Barcelona School of Architecture, but found its academic approach unrewarding and instead attended lectures on history, economics and philosophy, at the same time avidly reading Ruskin and exploring the Catalan countryside for its wealth of Romanesque and Gothic buildings. From the first he saw the architect as geometer, sculptor, painter, cabinet-maker, iron-worker and sociologist ...

Gaudí has been criticized by architects tied to the modern idiom of the right angle and the long straight line, and Oriol Bohigas, a leading practitioner of modern architecture in Barcelona, said of him: 'He lost interest in the new possibilities of iron, for example, and is merely the last great builder in stone.' Against this one may set a passage from Salvador Dalí's *The Visible Woman*:

> No collective effort has managed to create a dream world as pure and troubling as those Art Nouveau buildings which, on the fringe of architecture, alone constitute true realisations of solidified desires, in which suspension of conscious thought leads to hatred of reality and the need to find refuge in an ideal world ...

Gaudí sought to base both structure and ornament on freer natural forms, as opposed to geometrical planes and volumes. For example, the columns in his buildings resemble trees in that they taper towards the top, then branch out in different directions, to carry the weight of the vault. And, as with living organisms, the structure always conforms to mechanical principles. Without its many buttresses the nave of a Gothic cathedral would split open and collapse: in Gaudí's buildings the forces and thrusts are contained and channelled through sloping parabolic arches. His method was to make an upside-down model of the building by hanging small weights in appropriate places on cords fixed at either end to a horizontal base. According to the tension on them, the cords took up the shape of vaults, arches etc. If the shapes thus created were inverted, the forces would act in exactly the same way but in the opposite direction and the arch or vault would be self-supporting.

Antonio Gaudí's
unfinished Sagrada
Família in Barcelona

This is simple in principle; but to make the model establishing the lines of force for the church of the Colonia Güell, with string (woven into nets to represent the vaults), bags of lead shot, and stiff cloth to represent the walls, took his assistant, Francisco Berenguer, ten years. The result, with its lines of sloping parabolic piers, was a triumphant success and served as Gaudí's architectural laboratory for his transcendental project, the Cathedral of the Sagrada Família in Barcelona.

Most of Gaudí's work was undertaken for Count Eusebio Güell, a wealthy industrialist and patron in the manner of the Medicis. Among the works he commissioned were the Palacio Güell (1885–89), his Barcelona residence; the Parc Güell (1900–14) with its pavilion and sculptures decorated in glittering polychrome ceramic; and the church of the Colonia Güell (1898–1914), a village on the outskirts of the city intended for the workers in his cotton mills.

Notable buildings in Barcelona for other clients were the Casa Vicens (1883–85), with brickwork and tile in the Moorish Mudejar style; Casa Calvet (1898–1904), incorporating

43

baroque-style ironwork and naturalistic ornament in the form of fruit and mushrooms; Casa Batlló (1905–07), the so-called 'House of Skeletons', with its scaly, undulating roof and remarkable interior ornamentation; and Casa Milà (1905–10), on which the horizontal lines of the frontage resemble the waves of the Mediterranean.

Gaudí was thirty-one in 1883 when he took over the commission to supervise the construction of the Sagrada Família from the architect Joan Martorell, to whom he had been assistant. At the time he was somewhat of a dandy, outgoing and sociable. Ten years later the strain of the vast project was telling on him, and it was only a growing and exalted belief in the Catholic religion which gave him the inspiration and the faith to continue. The artist Opisso described him at the period as 'clothed like a beggar, with his white brow covered with curly locks falling from beneath his large black hat, defying the world, yet prouder and mightier than a Moorish king.'

Work on the huge structure progressed, and still progresses, as the result of collaboration between a team of architects and a host of sculptors and masons. It stopped only during the Spanish Civil War. Long before his untimely death, Gaudí knew that he would not live to see the temple completed. However, he left a large quantity of drawings and models, and although some were destroyed at the time of the Civil War, enough remain for the project to be carried through as he envisaged it. His plan involved three main façades: the Passion or Death, facing the Plaça de la Sagrada Família and flanked by the 138m (450 ft) towers which have made the building famous; the Nativity at the opposite side; and the unfinished Gloria, planned as the main entrance, with fountains shooting water 20m (65 ft) into the air at one side of the esplanade and, balancing them on the other, a huge torch, burning day and night and symbolizing the column of fire that led the Israelites into the desert. His designs also called for a huge central tower, 60m (200 ft) higher than the others.

Work has continued under the supervision of Gaudí's original team and their descendants, slowly at times for lack of funds, and more recently at accelerated pace. The principal architect, Jordi Bonet Armengol, son of one of Gaudí's trusted assistants, expects the nave to be roofed by the mid 1990s.

Gaudí himself died in June 1926. Absorbed in his schemes, he stumbled in front of a tramcar and was crushed by the wheels. Dressed in worn-out clothes and a threadbare jacket, he was at first taken for a beggar and moved to hospital; it was not until hours later that he was identified as one of the world's most famous architects. Opinions about the Sagrada Família have been mixed. The famous writer Miguel Unamuno strode about the site intoning in Castilian, 'No me gusta! No me gusta!' ('I don't like it!'), with Gaudí at his heels echoing him satirically in Catalan, 'No li agrada! No li agrada!' ('He doesn't like it!'); while George Orwell compared the towers to hock bottles. Perhaps more just and certainly more inspired are the lines from Jacint Verdaguer's L'Atlàntida:

Allà d'allà, per entre falgueres gegantines,
De sos menhirs y torres blanqueja l'ample front,
De marbres sobre marbres piràmides alpines
Que volent ab llurs testes omplir lo cel pregon.

There in front, between gigantic ferns,
See the wide white façade of menhirs and towers,
Marble upon marble in alpine pyramids,
Whose summits seem to pierce the sky.

Architecture continues to be a subject of intense interest in Barcelona, with leading architects receiving the coverage on television and in newspapers reserved for sports stars in less civilized climes. The cult figure of the 1960s was Ricardo Bofill, whose striking brick-built apartment block, Walden 7, is set back from the autopista to the south, for all the world like a gigantic, larger-than-life-sized Lego model. Most influential of modern architects have been Oriol Bohigas and his partners Josep Martorell and the English David Mackay, whose great achievement is not, perhaps, so much in individual buildings, simple and functional as they are, but in persuading the City Council to implement their plan for creating gardens, parks and squares, adorned with sculpture and ornamental water, in one of the most densely populated cities of Europe.

MODERN PAINTING AND LITERATURE

Modern Catalan painting has its roots in the Modernism (Modernisme) of the late nineteenth and early twentieth centuries. Santiago Rusiñol (1861–1932) was much admired by Gaudí. He and the other leading painter of the period, Ramon Casas (1866–1931), spent time in Paris, where they shared a studio with Maurice Utrillo. Like Utrillo, they were much influenced by the Impressionists, but developed along individual lines; in the main, Casas painted portraits and Rusiñol gardens, but the quality and range of their work may be appreciated in the Museu d'Art Modern in Barcelona. Casas was an extremely gifted lithographer and produced colourful and imaginative posters, reminiscent of those of Jules Chéret

45

and Toulouse Lautrec, for the *cava* house of Codorníu and Vicente Bosch, makers of Anís del Mono.

Casas and Rusiñol frequented a bar, Els Quatre Gats, part of a building in the Modernistic style designed by Puig i Cadafalch, which, at a time when Barcelona was in a creative ferment, became the hang-out of artists and architects (it still survives as a restaurant in the Carrer Montsió). Other regulars, apart from its founder Pere Romeu, were Ricardo Canals, Joaquin Mir, Miguel Utrillo, Oriol Martí and Ramon Pitxot. It was here that the young Picasso staged his first exhibition in 1900 and met the talented Isidro Nonell, with whom he was to share a studio in Paris during 1900–01, and also his life-long friend Jaume Sabartés who played a leading part in founding the Picasso Museum in Barcelona.

Picasso, in common with his famous friends and contemporaries, Joan Miró and Salvador Dalí, spent his early years as an artist in Catalonia. All three subsequently left for Paris, the magnet for Catalan painters of the period, and it was there that they found themselves and that their talents exploded. Because of their rooted antagonism to Franco and his regime, Picasso and Miró continued to work abroad, and only Dalí spent a major part of his career in Catalonia. Nevertheless, there is an unmistakable Catalan element in their painting, and the country has claimed them for her own with museums in their honour.

Pablo Picasso was born in Málaga, where his father was a teacher at the Fine Arts School. He was fourteen in 1895 when his father took up a post at the Llotja School of Art in Barcelona and the family moved there. Picasso, though under age, was entered as a student. He soon left the school; his father rented him his first studio and, apart from extended visits to Madrid and Paris, he spent most of his time in Barcelona until April 1904 when he left to live in Paris. He returned to Spain for holidays at Horta de Sant Joan near Tarragona and at Cadaqués, in 1910, where he spent the summer with Fernande Olivier and André Derain, and his last visit of any length to Barcelona was in 1917 with the Diaghilev ballet company. The Picasso Museum in Barcelona is particularly rich in his early work and of great interest in showing his development as a painter from childhood.

Miró was Catalan born and bred. Like Picasso, he attended the Llotja School of Art, but from the beginning he found drawing difficult, and it was largely on his own at his parents' house on the sea near Tarragona that he began experimenting with colour. Only later in Paris did he develop his own most individual style of surrealism with bright colours, flat shapes, and abstract patterns. Miró was as set on going to Paris as his Catalan contemporaries and was befriended there by Picasso, who bought paintings from him. He was as antagonistic to the Franquists as was Picasso and did not return to Spain until after the outbreak of World War II, living and working mainly in Mallorca but still bitterly opposed to the regime. The museum on Montjuïc, the Fundació Miró, an elegant modern building designed by his friend the architect Josep Lluis Sert (who emigrated to America as a protest against Franco and became Dean of Architectural Studies at Harvard University), contains two rooms of his early work, but the best of the paintings are of his late period, with fluid, fragmented images, drawn from the world of dreams and the subconscious, yet with all the gaiety and brightness of colour that were so inimitably his.

When Salvador Dalí in his turn arrived in Paris in the 1920s, he was greatly helped by his compatriot Miró, who introduced him to his agent, as also by Picasso. From the outset Dalí, though a very solid painter, was a flamboyant exhibitionist and a complete contrast to the reserved Miró. I myself [J.R.] remember going to his studio at Portlligat near Cadaqués to help make a documentary film about him. One of the stunts on which he insisted was that we hired a helicopter, attached ropes to his famous moustachios and hauled him into the air; a less likeable attribute was his habit of impaling fish against a virgin canvas so as to make patterns with their blood.

Dalí largely became famous in the United States where he not only painted for private patrons, but designed jewelry and arranged window displays for stores on Fifth Avenue in New York. Born in Figueres in 1901, he was the only one of the trio of painters without qualms about the Franco regime, and he spent long years painting in Spain. With his wife Gala, who had left the French surrealist poet Paul Eluard to marry him, he returned from America after the Civil War and painted at Portlligat amid an entourage of female disciples. His museum in Figueres, created by himself during his lifetime, is entirely unlike the scholarly institutions devoted to Miró and Picasso, and more in the nature of a jokey theatrical set. It was here that, ill and deserted, he spent his last years and is buried.

The leading painter of a younger generation is Antoni Tàpies, an innovator like Miró — and like Miró opposed to Franco and his regime — who has used paint in his own style to fathom the human mind. He has used his foundation in the Eixample in Barcelona to exhibit not only his own work but that of young and promising artists. His most eye-catching work is a great glass box containing a bizarre assortment of old furniture and sheets, located in a pool by the Parc de la Ciutadella. Entitled 'Homage to Picasso', it is the city's unexpected way of honouring one of its most unpredictable sons.

The relaxation of the ban on the Catalan language saw a flowering of Catalan literature. One of the first and most telling novels of the new wave was Fransesc Candil's best-selling *Els altres catalans*, written in 1964 about the plight of the under-privileged *xarnegos*, the immigrant workers from other parts of Spain. Among other influential writers, the temperamental Josep Pla (1897–1981) often wrote about his native Costa Brava. Mercè Rodoreda's finest novel, *La Plaça del Diamant*, set in Barcelona at the time of the Civil War, has been translated into English and is available in paperback, in Britain as *The Pigeon Girl* and in the USA as *The Time of Doves*. Another book available in English, first published in Barcelona by Seix Barral, a house which has done much to stimulate creative writing in Catalonia, is Eduardo Mendoza's *City of Miracles* (*La ciudad de los prodigios*), an epic account of life in Barcelona during a period of change and ferment from the 1880s to the 1920s. Other popular writers are Pere Gimferrer; Montserrat Roig; Quim Monzó; Manuel Vázquez Montalban, who writes detective stories with a Barcelona background; and Manuel de Pedrolo, who has written detective stories, science fiction and *avant-garde*, and whose *Mecanoscrit del segon origen* (*Draft of a Typescript*) has sold more than a quarter of a million copies.

MUSIC, DANCE AND FESTIVALS

The most prestigious symbol of the Catalan love for music is the Gran Teatre del Liceu in Barcelona. The original building, planned as an opera house second in size only to La Scala in Milan, opened in 1847, but was badly damaged by fire and restored and redecorated in 1862 by a team of painters headed by Josep Mirabent i Gatel. Social classes were strictly segregated, and for anyone who was anybody in nineteenth and early twentieth-century Barcelona possession of a family box was essential. Many of the greatest composers and singers have appeared at the Liceu, including Stravinsky, Falla and Albeniz, Caruso, Callas, Victoria de Los Angeles, and Catalan artistes such as Pau Casals, Montserrat Caballé and Josep Carreras. Today, the Liceu, which is being renovated and refitted for re-opening in 1992, is one of the great outposts in the revival of opera.

The other centre for music in Barcelona is Lluis Domenech i Montaner's extraordinary *fin de siècle* Palau de la Música, home of the Orféo Català (Catalan Choral Society), which also stages

Gran Teatre del Liceu,
Barcelona's impressive
19th-century opera
house

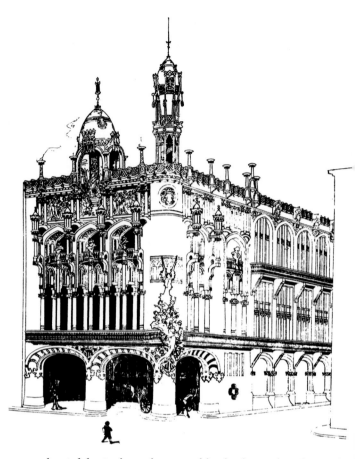

a number of festivals each year of both classical and popular music.

Apart from such festivals, every town and village in Catalonia has its own *festa major*, celebrated on the local saint's day, of which an indispensable ingredient is the dancing of the *sardana*. Although *sardana* in its present form emerged during the nineteenth century and the *Renaixença*, it had become so much a symbol of national identity that it was banned during the Franco period. It is danced in a ring, with the participants holding hands high in the air and stepping this way and that. Couples can join in at any point, but cannot cut in between a man and his partner on the right.

The *cobla* or band which plays the music for the dance consists of eleven players, and is made up of woodwind and brass, together with a double bass. This combination dates only from the *Renaixença* and was the invention of Pep Ventura, of a family from the Figueres area, who took advantage of the recently developed oboe-like *tenora* to banish the then popular bagpipes and develop a two-section band. Ventura adapted traditional Catalan songs for *sardana* as well as composing some of his own, including *El Cant dels Ocells*, often played by the cellist Pau Casals. The most celebrated *cobla* band, and the official band of the Generalitat, is La Principal from La Bisbal near Girona.

Characteristic of the local *festes* are the giants (*gegants*), huge papier-mâché figures sometimes 4.5m (15 ft) high, with copious skirts hiding the human performer inside. Giants always appear in couples, often as a king and queen, and are accompanied by *nans* or *capgrosses*, dancers with grotesque papier-mâché heads, who act as attendants and jesters. Another feature of some local festivals are the human towers (*castells*), of young men in traditional costume (*xiquets*), standing on each other's shoulders and several 'storeys' high. These are particularly impressive at Valls near Tarragona and at Vilafranca del Penedès.

Apart from local *festes* held on saints' days, there are others, such as Christmas, Twelfth Night, Holy Week and Easter, which are celebrated all over Spain and Catalonia. As in Spain generally, the Catalans make more of Twelfth Night, known as *Dia dels Reis* (Day of the Kings) than Christmas. It is then that children put out shoes at the window to be filled with presents brought by the three Magi from the East; and a special *tortell de reis*, a fancy bread in the form of a large ring, containing

OVERLEAF
Cakes and sweetmeats in a shop in Girona, specially made in the Catalan colours for St George's Day (Sant Jordi)

BELOW LEFT
Dancing the *sardana* during electioneering in Vilafranca del Penedès

BELOW RIGHT
Castell or human tower

candied fruit and a small token bringing luck to the person who finds it, is baked for the occasion. *Setmana Santa* (Holy Week preceding Easter) is the most important festival of the year. Although the ceremonies are not on the scale of those in Sevilla and Andalucía, many towns have processions, which are particularly impressive in Girona and Barcelona as they wind through the narrow streets around the cathedral. In other places, such as the former university town of Cervera, there are passion plays.

St George's Day (Sant Jordi – *see* page 9) is a day of dragons (*dracs*), red roses and books; a present of a rose and a book on St George's Day is an old tradition in Catalonia. Stalls are set up in the streets, and the Catalan gallant may also buy for his enamoured cakes and sweetmeats specially baked in the striped red and yellow of the Catalan flag.

The dragons, which are paraded around the streets like the *gegants* and *nans*, sometimes belching smoke and fire from their mouths, wings and tails, are of course part of the legend of the knight on the shining white horse and his rescue of the damsel. Like the *gegants* and *nans* the dragons are the proud possessions of the towns. The oldest in Catalonia, sometimes said to date from the last part of the fifteenth century but first recorded in the *Llibre Verd* in 1602, belongs to Vilafranca del Penedès. Originally made by the Gremi de Sabaters (Shoemakers' Guild) of wood, cardboard, hide, paper and horsehair, it has currently been hospitalized and is undergoing restorative treatment in Barcelona. Earlier in its life the dragon was customarily paraded by one Xemeni, the only person who could make an exact circle on the ground with its snout when dancing it. Xemeni, however, was drunk all year round, so that the mayor had to summon up his authority and declare on behalf of the citizens: 'Dance the dragon or go to prison!'

Dragons are a preoccupation of Barcelona and occur repeatedly in the city's architecture, from the Gothic cathedral to no less than three of Gaudí's most famous works – as the multicoloured ceramic beast of the Parc Güell, on the scaly roof of the Casa Batlló and in wrought iron on the gates of the Finca Güell. But these are not fierce dragons that eat damsels, but rather watchful custodians, perhaps evoked by Gaudí's friend, the poet Jacint Verdaguer, who wrote in his poem *L'Atlàndida* of the dragon who stood guard over the Gardens of Hesperides.

III · The Country

Rather than attempt a formal description of the places and countryside in Catalonia province by province, we have covered the ground rather differently with sections on the holiday coasts of the Costa Brava north of Barcelona and the Costa Daurada to its south; the Catalan Pyrenees; and the inland areas broadly north and south of Barcelona. There is a Catalan saying that Barcelona *is* Catalonia – meaning that the city has always dominated the region's history, culture and commerce – and Barcelona therefore has an extended section of its own.

THE COSTA BRAVA

About the time when I [J.R.] first visited the Costa Brava, that enterprising and erudite traveller Rose Macaulay wrote in her *Fabled Shore* (1949):

> The road, the old Roman road from Gaul to Tarragona, sweeps up from Port Bou in wild and noble curves, lying like a curled snake along the barren mountain flanks of the Alta Ampurdan, climbing dizzily up, darting steeply down into gorges and ravines, above deep rocky inlets where blue water thrusts into rock-bound coves, and small bays of sand where it whispers and croons in its tideless stir. Points and capes jut boldly through thin blue air above a deep cobalt sea; rocky islets lie offshore, the road dips down ...

That is how in the mind's eye one sees the Costa Brava (the name means 'wild coast'), however much parts of it may now have been built on and ravaged.

Even in Rose Macaulay's time, the coastal route north from Barcelona along the N11, through what is called **El Maresme**, passed through ugly industrial suburbs and then along a dullish stretch of road, which, together with the railway line, cuts off the towns from their beaches and the sea. Today, the landscape has a somewhat lunar look, with what turn out to be, not space colonies, but huge plastic greenhouses, supplying fruit and vegetables to Barcelona. Nevertheless, **El Masnou, Premià de Mar** and **Arenys de Mar** have beaches and marinas and are popular at weekends and in the summer with the Barceloneses. The port and marina at Arenys de Mar, with rank on rank of moored yachts and a maze of masts, spars and cordage against the sky, are particularly attractive.

Sailing is a national pastime of the Catalans. We know couples who depart from Barcelona every weekend – except in the depths of winter or when the Tramuntana, swooping down from the Pyrenees, confines even large craft to harbour – and make for the spot along the Costa Brava or the Costa Daurada where their boat is moored. And like it (or pretend to like it) or not, the wife must set to with cooking *tortillas* for on-board provisions and hauling up sails, come rain come shine, until her hands are raw. With some 480 km of coastline and thirty-six marinas (*see* maps of the Costa Brava and Costa Daurada, pp. 58 and 113, for the main ones), these are ideal waters for sailing, and on the Costa Brava there are many enchanting coves and beaches which can be approached only from the sea. Races for different classes of craft are organized throughout the year. Details may be had from the Federació Catalana de Vela (Catalan Sailing Federation) of Barcelona. Masnou is one of the most important centres for chandlers and for chartering yachts, and the largest marina is situated on the 15 km of canals around the new resort of Santa Margarida near Roses. Advice and help in planning itineraries may be obtained from the Associació de Crucers (National Cruising Association) in Barcelona, which has affiliates all along the coast.

The Costa Brava proper begins with **Blanes** and **Lloret de Mar**. When I first visited them, the narrow and dusty main road wound through a row of fishermen's houses and small shops. Former fishing villages, they are now the headquarters of the package tour, with discos, souvenir and fast food shops side by side. Lloret is said to possess more hotels than any other resort in Spain, but there is also a handsome palm-fringed promenade and wide beach with fine sand.

Once through Lloret the coast road, now the GE 682, climbs steeply above the shore and for the next 34 km of corniche as far as Sant Feliu it runs high above the red cliffs, twisting and turning through luxuriant groves of pine and cork oak, with sudden views of jutting headlands, secret beaches and small coves, the water changing in colour from emerald green to cobalt. At intervals it swoops down to circle a deeper inlet at shore level and some halfway to Sant Feliu descends steeply into **Tossa de Mar**. Shut in by wooded hills, with a curving beach dominated at one end by a twelfth-century tower and walls, Tossa was a picture book fishing village when it was first 'discovered' by writers and artists (among them Marc Chagall) before World War II. It has survived the tourist influx of the last decades better than many places, and though the row of

Catalonia: general map

old houses on the front has been swept away by the hard horizontal lines of a modern concrete hotel, the old streets behind still remain.

The sizeable town of **Sant Feliu de Guixols** was once the centre of a flourishing cork trade (the subsequent decline of the trade is well described in Norman Lewis's evocative novel *Voices of the Old Sea*). Its former importance is echoed by the locomotive on the front, which once plied on a now abandoned line to Girona, and the size of the port, the most important on

The Costa Brava

FRANCE

Cerbere
Portbou
Colera
El Port de Llançà
Llançà
El Port de la Selva
Cadaquès
Sant Pere de Rodes
Roses
Muga
Perelada
Castelló d'Empúries
Figueres
Fluvia
Empúries
L'Escala

COSTA BRAVA

L'Estartit
Torroella de Montgrí
MEDES IS
Ter
Sa Riera
Ullastret
Begur
Pals
Peratallada
Fornells
Aiguablava
Tamariu
La Bisbal
Palafrugell
Llafranc
Calella
GIRONA
Palamós
Platja d'Aro
S'Agaró
St Feliu de Guixols
Sils
Tossa del Mar
Roca Grossa
Lloret de Mar
Tordera
Tordera
Blanes
Arenys de Mar
Premià de Mar
El Masnou

N

kilometres
0   15

the Costa Brava until the construction of marinas up and down the coast. Sant Feliu is now a popular holiday resort and home of the original Eldorado Petit restaurant (its creator, Luís Cruanyas, who is from Sant Feliu, later started offshoots in Barcelona and New York).

OVERLEAF
Marina at Arenys de
Mar on the Maresme

At **S'Agaró**, on the cliffs beyond Sant Feliu, there is the most up-market development on the coast with luxurious villas and well-kept gardens, also the first of the Costa Brava's luxury hotels, the Hostal de la Gavina. It was built in 1923 by a Catalan industrialist, Josep Ensesa, as a small 15-room hotel. He encouraged friends and associates to build villas around it in the same style and also cut a promenade along the cliffs. Even before the Spanish Civil War it was attracting the fashionable crowd from the French Riviera, and when Ensesa extended it after the war, it became famous because of the visits of film stars such as Ava Gardner, Frank Sinatra, Orson Welles, Elizabeth Taylor and Montgomery Clift. The Spanish surgeon, Professor Josep Trueta, who practised in Oxford and London, also sang its praises to illustrious patients such as Winston Churchill and Aristotle Onassis. Rose Macaulay says rather acidly that she is 'sure that life there must be very comfortable, sociable and classy,' but that 'I would not stay there myself, even had I the necessary pesetas.' If *very* expensive, we still recommend visiting it for the experience.

A few kilometres on along the C253, as the coast road now becomes, is **La Platja d'Aro**. 'Platja' means 'playa', and the beach here *is* long and sandy; otherwise the place is a mass of concrete and discos, relieved only by Carles Camos's Big Rock restaurant, serving first-rate Catalan dishes and installed in an old hill-top house.

At **Palamós**, founded in 1279 by Pere (Peter) II ('The Great'), a fishing port which also stages sailing events during the year, the road turns inland for **Palafrugell**, the birthplace of the celebrated Catalan writer Josep Pla and a centre of the cork trade. From Palafrugell there are country roads down to a cluster of pretty villages and beaches: **Calella**; **Llafranc**; **Tamariu**; **Aiguablava**, where a white modern Parador looks down into the blue water of a deeply indented cove; and **Begur**. Off the road to Calella are the Botanical Gardens of Cap Roig. Constructed by a White Russian colonel and his English wife, the glowing flowers and Mediterranean shrubs grow on terraces poised above a sunlit sea.

Northwards from Palafrugell, the landscape changes, the wooded hills giving way to the broad coastal plain of Empordà. The most interesting route north is by the GE650 to Pals and Torroella de Montgrí. **Pals**, once a port in a rice-growing area,

but now well inland, has well-preserved medieval walls and towers, a Gothic church, and is dominated by its old castle, the Torre de les Hores. It also boasts a good restaurant with sophisticated Catalan cookery in Sa Punta. Of even more historic interest is the little walled town of **Peratallada** (a short diversion inland beyond Pals by the GE651). Built on live rock cleft by deep gullies, its narrow streets converge on the main square and a Romanesque church. The castle dates from the eleventh century and the palace is built around a courtyard, part Romanesque, part Gothic. **Ullastret**, a few kilometres further on, also has its medieval precinct, but is best known for the neighbouring site of an Iberian town of the fourth to third centuries BC. It has been carefully excavated to reveal the remains of walls and houses, and the square resembles those of certain Greek settlements.

North of Pals on the GE650, **Torroella de Montgrí** on the River Ter, 9 km on, is another place of great historic interest. The ancient castle of the Kings of Aragon was a favourite residence of Joan I at the end of the fourteenth century (it now forms the site of an elegant Modernist building, the Mirador). There are also old walls, a colonnaded square, baronial houses and a Gothic church, the venue for an international music festival. The massive Castle of Montgrí above the town was built by Jaume II ('The Conqueror') to keep in check the turbulent Counts of Empúries.

L'Estartit, a small fishing port and holiday resort near the mouth of the river Ter 5 km from Torroella, is the embarkation point for the glass-bottomed boats taking visitors out to the **Medes Islands**. A couple of kilometres offshore and once a pirates' lair, the islands now mark a marine reserve established in 1985. Another has recently been set up around the underwater pinnacles of Els Ullastres 15 km further south. In spite of angry protests from local fishermen, the conservation measures came in the nick of time because the inshore waters had been fished out to meet the consumption of the armies of summer tourists. Coral, too, had been ruthlessly dragged from the rocks, first by fishermen and later from the mouths of underwater caves by aqualung divers.

Thanks to measures taken by the government's agriculture and fisheries department, which prohibit the removal of any living growth within an area of seventy-five metres around the islands, aqualung divers report that the sea in the vicinity is now teeming with fish of all sorts, including anchovy, sardines, bass, barracuda, sea flies and gilthead, to name a few. Diving is becoming increasingly popular and diving centres and schools have been set up in resorts along the coast such as L'Estartit,

Llafranc, Roses, Cadaqués and a dozen more. A permit from the local marine commandant is necessary, and this may be obtained through these centres.

North of Torroella, **L'Escala** at the southern end of the Gulf of Roses is famous for its salted anchovies – though its sandy beaches have now made it more of a holiday resort than a fishing port. L'Escala is only 2 km from the ruins of the Graeco-Roman city of **Empúries**. They lie behind groves of pine trees just back from a wide, sandy beach with a vista of the azure curve of the Gulf of Roses and Roses itself on the far shore. The precinct, with its cypress trees, broken columns, honey-coloured masonry and tesselated paving, is fenced off, and to avoid disappointment do *not* turn up on a Monday (visiting hours on other days: April to September, 10.00 to 14.00 and 15.00 to 19.00; rest of the year, 10.00 to 13.00 and 15.00 to 17.00).

The Greeks first arrived from Massalia (Marseille) towards the middle of the sixth century BC to found the trading settlement of Emporion ('the market'). This first settlement, known as Palaiapolis ('the old city'), was on the islet of Sant Martí, now joined to the shore. Since this was built over in medieval times and is now the village of Sant Martí d'Empúries, it has been little excavated. Excavation of the second and larger Greek settlement of Neapolis and of the later Roman city of Emporiae has been proceeding since 1908. It has proved extremely difficult because of the superposition of buildings constructed over some 1000 years.

Livy, writing some two centuries after the landing of the Romans under Gnaeus Cornelius Scipio at Empúries in 218 BC and quoted by Rose Macaulay in *Fabled Shore*, gives a very clear account of the layout of the city as it existed in his time:

Even at that time [195 BC, when Cato landed there with army and fleet] Emporiae consisted of two towns separated by a wall. One was inhabited by Greeks from Phocaea (whence came the Massilienses also) the other by the Spaniards; but the Greek town, being entirely open to the sea, had only a small extent of wall, while the Spaniards, who were further back from the sea, had a wall three miles round. A third class of inhabitants, Roman colonists, was added by the deified Caesar ... The part of the wall which faced the interior they [the Greeks] kept strongly fortified, with only a single gate ... Through the gate which led to the Spanish town they never passed except in large bodies ... The cause of going out of the town was this: the Spaniards, who had no experience with the sea, enjoyed transacting business with them, and wanted both to buy the foreign merchandise which they brought in their ships, and to dispose of the products of their own farms. The desire of the

63

benefits of this interchange caused the Spanish city to be open to the Greeks.

Much of the massive wall with its single gate survives, together with the rectangular grid of crossing streets and open squares of this little city of sea breezes and the sound of the sea. Among the ruins are the temples of Asclepius, god of medicine, and of Zeus Serapis; a watch tower; water cisterns with a reconstructed filter; the *agora* or main square; and in a street leading down to the sea, the *stoa*, a covered market with the remains of shops and an arcade where traders bought and sold.

With the coming of the Romans, the Greeks became allies and on the rising ground beyond the Greek city Emporion was greatly enlarged into Roman Empuriae. Excavations, still incomplete, have revealed the walls; villas; mosaic pavements; a forum flanked by shops, temples and an arcade; and outside the walls a large oval amphitheatre.

Because it was at Empúries that the Greeks first set foot in Spain, it is here that the Olympic flame will be brought from Athens to inaugurate the 1992 Games in Barcelona.

If, taking leave of Emporion and its Graecian ghosts, one heads north for Roses, the road goes by way of **Castelló d'Empúries**, once the capital of the Counts of Empordà. There are the remains of past splendours in the shape of the fourteenth-century church of Santa Maria, with its beautiful sculptured portico and fine tower, and also old houses and a medieval bridge. Between Castello d'Empúries and Roses, on the verge of the new resort of Santa Margarida, with its high-rise apartments built on reclaimed marshland around a network of canals, lies the **Parc Natural de las Zonas Humedas del Empordà**, a wetland nature reserve, especially interesting as a refuge for migratory birds.

Roses, at the northern end of the Gulf of Roses, was founded by Greek mariners from Rhodes, who named it after their home. It was fortified in the sixteenth century by the Emperor Charles V, who constructed the citadel as a bastion against the Turks. The outlying fort of La Trinitat was built to protect the port and was the object of a fierce attack by the French during the Peninsular War. For cool and insolent daring its defence by the British naval commander, Lord Cochrane, was one of the outstanding combined operations of the war; it was vividly recorded by Captain Marryat, who served under Cochrane as a midshipman on the *Impérieuse*, in his novel *Frank Mildmay*.

Having ascertained that the French artillery was so placed that it could not hole the tower less than sixty feet above ground, Cochrane, in his own words, 'constructed a huge

OPPOSITE
Pavilion in the Parc Guell in Barcelona designed by Antonio Gaudí

OVERLEAF ABOVE LEFT
The rocky coast of the Costa Brava

OVERLEAF BELOW LEFT
Cadaqués, the unspoilt village on the Costa Brava, where Salvador Dalí first painted

OVERLEAF RIGHT
A street in Cadaqués

wooden case, exactly resembling the hopper of a mill – the upper part being kept well greased with cook's slush from the *Impérieuse*, so that to retain a hold upon it was impossible. Down this, with the slightest pressure from behind, the storming party must have fallen to a depth of fifty feet, and all they could have done, if not killed, would have been to remain prisoners at the bottom of the bomb proof.' When the French launched an all out attack on 30 November 1808 with some 1,200 men they were repulsed with heavy loss by a handful of sailors from the frigate. Cochrane himself had earlier been 'struck by a stone splinter in the face; the splinter flattening my nose and then penetrating my mouth. By the skill of our excellent doctor, Mr. Guthrie, my nose was after a time rendered serviceable.' The stubborn defence of Roses was in the end unavailing, but held up the French advance on Barcelona by a month.

Roses is today surrounded, not by Napoleonic invaders, but by all the amenities of mass tourism – supermarkets, discos, aquaparks and go-kart tracks. There could not be a more complete contrast than **Cadaqués**, only a short distance to the north, but on the road to nowhere else on the peninsula of Cap de Creus, the most easterly point of the Spanish coast and in the past virtually inaccessible except by boat. Shut in by mountains, a cluster of white houses overlooking the bluest of bays, it is dominated by a great Baroque church and its cobbled alleys run steeply up and down hill. Crowded in summer, it has so far escaped the construction of high-rise apartments and large hotels and still preserves something of the atmosphere of an artists' colony with a clutch of sophisticated private galleries as well as Dalí museums. It was here that Picasso painted some famous cubist canvases in 1910, and during the 1920s its most famous son, Salvador Dalí, attracted there a veritable role call of surrealists and others: Eluard, Magritte, Duchamp, Man Ray, Buñuel and Lorca. (If you run short of cobalt blue or turps, as I did, the small *ferreteria* (ironmonger) continues to stock a remarkable range of oil colours, brushes and artist's materials.) The hamlet of Portlligat, where Dalí painted from 1940, is a couple of kilometres up the coast, a tiny harbour with his studio just above it.

El Port de la Selva, 13 km north of Cadaqués by the GE613, sheltered at the end of its bay, is a small fishing port turned holiday resort, and when the wind blows (as it often does) an ideal place for windsurfing. From the bay the steepest of roads (there is an easier approach from Llançà further north and Vilajuiga inland of it) leads up to the monastery of **Sant Pere de Rodes**, one of the most magnificent of all the Romanesque buildings in Catalonia. High on a hillside, its ruined towers and walls command a breathtaking panorama of the Gulf of Lyon. Constructed by the Benedictines between 979 and 1022, it was sacked and abandoned in the eighteenth century and its bible is now in the Bibliothèque Nationale in Paris. Best preserved is the church at its centre with three wide naves and capitals delicately carved with acanthus leaves.

The last of the holiday resorts are **El Port de Llançà**, with a good beach, and **Colera**. From Llançà, one may either take the winding N260 northwards, zig zagging over the last spurs of the Pyrenees to **Portbou** and the French frontier or take the eastern branch to Figueres. Halfway to Figueres, at **Perelada**, the birthplace of the Catalan chronicler Muntaner, there is the impressive castle of the Rocaberti family dating from the sixteenth and seventeenth centuries, housing a museum of glass and ceramics, an important library, and an elegant casino.

OVERLEAF
The Vall d'Aran

Glass and ceramic
museum in the Castell
de Perelada

It is also the venue each summer of a well-known International Festival of Music. Adjacent to it the fourteenth-century Convent del Carme has a particularly beautiful cloister and patio, and underneath it run the cellars and interesting wine museum of the wine concern of the Castillo de Perelada. How better say *benvinguts* or *adéu* (welcome or goodbye) to Catalonia than with a glass of their sparkling *cava*!

THE CATALAN PYRENEES

The first view of the Pyrenees, from a plane en route to Barcelona, is also one of the most impressive: in winter, mile upon mile of glittering snow-covered peaks and ridges; and in summer, great hollowed green valleys with here and there a tiny road snaking up to a handful of houses or an isolated farm. It *is* perhaps from the air that one best understands how formidable a barrier these mountains have been throughout the history of Spain; and to this day parts of the region are among the most inaccessible in Europe, retaining traditional ways of life, slate-roofed houses and Romanesque churches, and forming a great natural nature reserve.

The Catalan Pyrenees are highest in the west, with Mount Aneto, just over the border into Aragon, topping 3400 m (11,000 ft), and fall away towards the Mediterranean, where the last spurs plunge into the sea at Cap de Creus. The main roads run from north to south down the river valleys – the Noguera Ribagorçana, Noguera Pallaresa, Segre, Llobregat, Freser and Ter – and cross country communications are scarce or non-existent. For this reason it is difficult to recommend a route through the area, but for those prepared for an, at times, switch-back ride, the described itinerary via Ripoll, Puigcerdà, La Seu d'Urgell, Tremp, Sort and the Vall d'Aran, takes in a representative swathe of this most beautiful region.

Ripoll may be approached either from Barcelona via Vic and the N152 (*see* p.91) or from France by the **Collado de Ares**, 1610 m (4830 ft). Between the pass and Ripoll the C151 first reaches **Camprodón**, a handsome town with a high-arched medieval bridge over the River Ter (licences for trout-fishing are available at the tourist office), old houses, good shops and a well-preserved Romanesque church. The road continues downhill past rushing streams and through wooded pasturage to **Sant Joan de les Abadesses**, a small, medieval town named after the first abbess of its tenth-century monastery, the daughter of Guifré el Pilós, founder of the House of Barcelona. Apart from the nave and elegant fifteenth-century cloister, the most remarkable feature of the church is the polychrome wooden

73

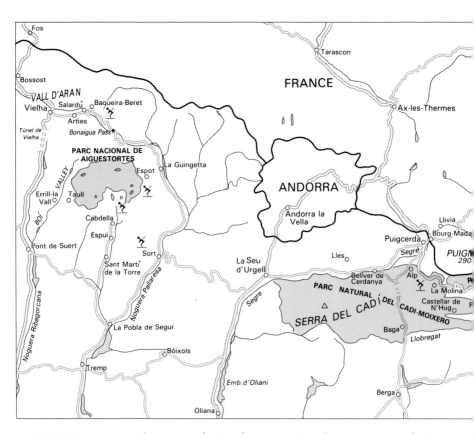

The Catalan Pyrenees

altarpiece, dating from 1251 and representing the Descent
from the Cross, and astonishing in the realism of its figures.

Ripoll, at the junction of the rivers Ter and Freser, has
sometimes been called the birthplace of the Catalan nation. Its
famous monastery was founded in the ninth century by Guifré
el Pilós and it was here until the twelfth century that the
Counts of Barcelona, Besalú and Cerdaña were buried. In the
eleventh century, under its powerful Abbot Oliba, the monastery, with one of the best libraries of Christendom, became an
outstanding centre of learning (*see* p.35). Unfortunately the
building was severely damaged by an earthquake in 1428 and
the destruction was completed in 1835 by anticlerics who set
fire to it. It has been carefully reconstructed, but the only part
of the original to survive is Oliba's magnificently carved porch.
In medieval times Ripoll was known for its forges worked by
water power, and in the local museum there is an interesting
exhibit illustrating the manufacture of nails and firearms.

From Ripoll the N152 follows the green valley of the Freser
up to **Ribes de Freser**, a small mountain resort from which a
rack and pinion railway affording magnificent views climbs up

the mountain side to **Núria**, a winter sports centre at some 1800 m (6000 ft) and also a favourite starting point for hikers to explore the nature reserve of Freser-Setcases. Beyond Ribes the road spirals dizzily up above a green and leafy valley, and over the pass there are wide views of the plain of the Cerdanya, a high plateau some 1220 m (4000 ft) above sea level divided by the frontier, since the northern part was ceded to France by the Treaty of the Pyrenees of 1659. Near the col a mountain road leads off to **La Molina** and **Super Molina**, the first and still among the most popular of ski stations in Catalonia.

The capital of the Cerdanya is the frontier town of **Puigcerdà** built on a low hill overlooking the plain. Although much damaged during the Civil War, it has kept some of its old balconied houses and is a prosperous market town selling fruit, vegetables and cheeses from the surrounding area. Six kilometres over the frontier along a 'neutral' stretch of road is a twelve-square-kilometre enclave of Spain in France. **Llivia** has remained Spanish because, when the Roselló (Roussillon) was made over to France in 1659, mention was made of its thirty-three villages, but not of its only town, Llivia. It possesses some picturesque old streets, a fortified church and a museum incorporating an old pharmacy which opened its doors in 1416 and closed in 1926.

From Puigcerdà the N260 to La Seu d'Urgell descends through the farmlands of the Cerdanya, a green landscape punctuated by groves of tall Lombardy poplars and huddled slate-roofed farmsteads to **Bellver de Cerdanya**, a town on the northern edge of the Parc Natural de Cadí-Moixeró (*see* p.85), where the tourist office will advise on walks through the park or arrange for the hire of Jeeps or Land Rovers. At Martinet, a by-road, with marvellous views of the peaks to the north and the Serra del Cadí to the south, leads up to **Lles**, situated 18 km to the north at a height of some 1370 m (4500 ft) in a great amphitheatre of mountains.

La Seu d'Urgell, where the N260 makes junction with the N145 into Andorra, is the most interesting town in the Catalan Pyrenees. Since 1278 the Bishops of Urgell have been joint-rulers of Andorra, first with the Counts of Foix and now with the President of France, and are the only remaining prelates with temporal authority. Their Cathedral of Santa Maria was built in the eleventh and twelfth centuries and displays marked Lombard influence. With its lofty nave and side aisles, its thirteenth-century cloister, the beautiful Chapel of Sant Miquel, the Romanesque statue of Santa Maria d'Urgell in the apse and treasures like the first ever map of the Pyrenees, it is most impressive. The town, a lively commercial and agricultural

Girona. Houses by the River Onyar

The promenade at Lloret de Mar

centre known for its manufacture of cheeses, nevertheless preserves much of its medieval atmosphere, and among the old houses is one which belonged to the last of the Anti-Popes, Pedro de Luna. There is a comfortable modern parador built on the site of the fourteenth-century church of Sant Domingo, which has preserved the old cloister as a striking indoor garden.

Southwards from La Seu d'Urgell the C1313 follows the Segre valley, passing through the rocky gorge of the Garganta de Tresports before reaching the top of the great reservoir of Oliana closed in by great grey rocks with cascades of water down the sides. At Coll de Nargó, the L511 branches off for Tremp, with a corniche climbing dizzily up to the **Coll de Bóixols** at 1370 m (4500 ft); the views across the mountains are spectacular, but this is a narrow and difficult road and not for the squeamish (an alternative route to the Vall d'Aran, longer but much faster, is by the C1313 to Lleida and then by the N230 and Vielha tunnel). **Tremp**, situated on a wide plain, has its old quarter, but is primarily a commercial centre for the hydro-electric industry and fruit trade. The N260 to the north skirts one of the reservoirs of the hydro-electric scheme and follows the valley of the Noguera Pallaresa into the mountains. At **Sort**, the N260 turns east for La Seu d'Urgell over another spectacular roller coaster. The C147 continues north, and 24 km on there is a turning for **Espot**, the entry point for the Parc Nacional de Aigüestortes. The road reaches its high point at the 2070 m (6500 ft) **Bonaigua Pass** (open, because of snow, only from April/May to October/November) surrounded by peaks, with the magnificent circle of a glacier on the left hand side. This is the entrance to the **Vall d'Aran**, which was almost isolated from the outside world until the opening of the pass in 1925. Even then, the pass was frequently blocked in winter, and regular communications were not established until the five-kilometre Vielha Tunnel was driven under the mountains in 1948.

Because of its long isolation the beautiful thirty-mile-long Vall d'Aran is one of the most unspoilt and individual enclaves in Spain and has largely preserved its traditions and dialect, which is nearer to Provençal than Catalan. The mountains, dazzlingly mantled with snow for much of the year, soar up on either side and the villages, thirty-nine in all, with their grey-slated granite houses, each clustered around its Romanesque church, hug the lower slopes or sit astride the Garona – the same majestic Garonne that flows into the Atlantic at Bordeaux but here an impetuous mountain stream.

In winter, Baqueira-Beret at the eastern end of the valley is now the most fashionable ski resort in Spain; in summer the meadows are enamelled with alpine flowers and skiers give way to climbers, hikers and fishermen. There are numbers of good hotels and sophisticated restaurants – closed out of season for part of May and June and again in November – to cope with this holiday activity, and also Paradores at Vielha and Arties open all year round.

Chalets on the road to Beret

After the descent of the Pass of Bonaigua, the first place is the ski resort of Baqueira, from which a good modern road spirals up to Beret. There are some two dozen different pistes, ranging from easy to very difficult, and a dozen ski lifts at Baqueira; fifteen pistes and half a dozen lifts at Beret; and another four pistes and three ski-lifts at Argulls, all controlled from a central communications tower. Everything else that a skier could want is available: ski hire, medical services, helicopter services to distant summits, ski schools for adults and children, a slalom stadium and Nordic skiing. Social life centres on Baqueira, where there are excellent hotels, restaurants and discos, constructed with considerable taste from local materials so that they do not disfigure the magnificent backdrop of mountains and fir trees. Many Spanish ski enthusiasts, including the Royal Family, have their own chalets and regularly drive up from Barcelona or Madrid during the season (from December to April).

Further down the valley, **Salardú** is a village of old grey houses with wooden balconies, an arcaded square and a thirteenth-century Romanesque church with a tall bell-tower; its wooden Christ dates from the twelfth century. **Arties**, built on both sides of the Garona, also has a pretty Romanesque church against a splendid mountain background – its door used

81

Romanesque church at
Salardú

as a noticeboard and advertising eggs when we were last there shows how much of the country these villages remain – though Casa Irene next to the Parador and much frequented by visitors from across the French border is one of the best and most sophisticated restaurants in Spain.

The capital of the Vall d'Aran is **Vielha**, a bustling resort town with a population of some 3000. Here you will find hotels and restaurants; sports shops and boutiques galore with everything for the skier; a riding stables; and a helpful tourist office with up-to-date information on the condition of the forest tracks. There is a large Parador just above the town and good skiing at La Tuca 5 km outside. The Church of Sant

Miquel has a thirteenth-century octagonal bell tower and conserves the wooden bust of the Mig Aran Christ, all that remains of a finely carved twelfth-century Descent from the Cross. At Bossost, 16 km from Vielha along a road with spectacular views of the snowy peaks of the Maladeta mountains, at the foot of the Portillo Pass into France and the last village in Spain, there is perhaps the most beautiful Romanesque church in the Aran valley. Its three naves are divided by arches and sturdy round pillars, which support a vaulted roof. The three apses are decorated with Lombard carving and the north doorway with carvings of the Creator, the sun and the moon, and the Evangelists.

RUTAS DEL ROMÁNICO

The Catalans are so deeply conscious of the influence on their culture of Romanesque art that the Departament de Comerç, Consum i Turisme publishes a comprehensive guide with maps of six 'Romanic Routes' covering the whole of Catalonia and every Romanesque building of importance. It would indeed be a devoted student of architecture who drove all of those '*itinerarios propuestos*', survived the '*pistas de montana*', and visited the hundreds of listed churches. One can see him in his dreams spinning off a mountain corniche and meeting his Creator with a vision of bell-towers and acanthus leaves. In all seriousness, the churches of this northwestern corner of the country are so unique as to make detours well worthwhile.

Two such may be made when returning from the Vall d'Aran down the main, well-engineered and fast road to Lleida (Lérida). Eight kilometres out of Vielha the N230 enters the Túnel de Vielha, five kilometres of dripping concrete and overhead lights. It then follows down the Noguera Ribagorçana river and a series of reservoirs, scenically contained between great folded strata of pink rock, and plays hide and seek in a succession of smaller tunnels until it reaches the hydro-electric centre of Pont de Suert. A few kilometres before Pont de Suert a road to the left leads up the mountainous Boí Valley. Surrounded by high mountains and with Parc Nacional de Aigüestortes (*see* p.84) just to the east, the valley possesses perhaps the finest cluster of twelfth- and thirteenth-century Romanesque churches in Catalonia: those of the villages of Cóll, Barruera, Durro, Boí, Erill-la-Vall and the two of Taüll. Splendid examples are Santa Eulalia in Errill-la Val and Sant Climent in Taüll, both with slender six-storey bell towers. The celebrated sculpture of the Descent from the Cross from Errill is now on display at the Museum of Catalan Arts in Barcelona. Sant

Climent, set in a green meadow among leafy trees with a blue mountainside rising steeply behind it, is now a museum. Perhaps the most famous of all these Romanesque churches, it was consecrated within a day of the other larger church in the centre of Taüll, that of Santa Maria, in 1123 (both being built by the noble family of Errill). It possesses three naves and apses. The beautiful murals of Christ, his saints and Apostles, and scenes from the Old and New Testaments and of the Apocalypse have been removed to the Museum of Catalan Arts, but have been replaced by a faithful reproduction.

Shortly after Pont de Suert another turning to the left, the C144, crosses the vantage point of the Coll de Perves, and at Senterada a further left turn leads to another group of Romanesque churches at **Sant Martí de la Torre**, Espui and **Cabdella**.

NATURE RESERVES

There are numbers of large nature reserves in the Catalan Pyrenees of which the most important are the Parc Nacional de Aigüestortes i Llac de Sant Maurici, the Parc Natural del Cadí-Moixeró and the Hunting Reserve of Freser-Setcases. All are open free to the public, but permitted activities inside the parks vary according to their legal status. Regulations are rigid at the National Park of Aigüestortes, where it is absolutely forbidden to hunt or to interfere with any type of wild life. Camping and fires are forbidden and access is by foot or by jeep, hired at a local hotel. Climbing is permitted, and there is also Nordic skiing in winter. At the Natural Park of Cadí-Moixeró, on the other hand, permits may be obtained for hunting and fishing in specified areas.

Aigüestortes

The park lies south of the Vall d'Aran and occupies some hundred square metres of glorious mountain scenery at a height of 1060–2130 m (3500–7000 ft) with peaks such as Colomes rising to 2900 m (9600 ft). It is called 'Aigüestortes' ('twisting waters') because of the hundreds of waterfalls cascading down the mountainsides and of the torrents feeding its tarns. It may be approached either from Caldes de Boí at the head of the Boí Valley (*see* p.83) in the east or from Espot (*see* p.80) on the western side. The road from Espot leads to the Lake of Sant Maurici, with the summits of the Serra de Encatats reflected in it. To cross the park on foot by the lake and the track through Portarro d'Espot, from which there are magnificent views, is a day's walk (there are refuges where one may spend the night).

Less energetic walkers may still see the pine and fir forests, the banks of red rhododendron in spring, the yellow and violet gentian, and glimpse a chamois gambolling on the rocky slopes. The breed was near extinction, but since the creation of the nature reserves numbers are much on the increase. The brown bear is almost extinct, but the fauna includes wild boar, golden eagles, woodpeckers and the rare and beautiful bearded vulture (known as *trancalos* or 'bone-breaker' in Catalan), which breeds in the park.

Cadí-Moixeró

The Serra del Cadí runs parallel to the Pyrenees and to the south, but its mountains are limestone, not granite. The natural park, with an area of 41 square kilometres and ranging in height from 610 m (2000 ft) valley bottoms to the 2648 m (8685 ft) peak of Canal Baridana, lies to the east of Aigües-tortes between La Seu d'Urgell and Ripoll. The information centre for the park is the tourist office at Bellver de Cerdanya (*see* p.77 – Bellver may also be approached direct via the 5-km tunnel on the C1411 from Barcelona).

Because of the low temperatures and high degree of humidity the fauna and flora in the park are more typical of northern and central Europe than of the Mediterranean. Pine and fir grow on the rocky mountain slopes up to heights of 1830–2135 m (6000–7000 ft) and the lower slopes are clothed with beech, chestnut and rhododendrons. There is a profusion of Alpine plants, and for the knowledgeable two of the jewels of the park are *Xatardia scabra* and *Ramonda myconi*, with its dark violet flowers and fleshy leaves. Among the fauna chamois are plentiful, and one may see deer and sable. There are golden eagles, capercailzie, the common and Alpine chough and, in the more distant fir and pine forests, Europe's largest woodpecker, the jet black *Dryocopus martius*.

Garrotxa Volcanic Park

The park, some 120 square kilometres in area, centres on the volcanic area around Olot (*see* p.89), the largest of the type in the Iberian Peninsula. The thirty volcanoes, of which some, like that of Santa Margarida between Olot and Santa Pau, are well-preserved, were first active some 350,000 years ago, with violent eruptions every 10,000 years. The last took place some 11,500 years ago – but as the official guide to the park puts it: 'This is a case of inactive volcanoes, which cannot be considered definitely extinguished.' Visitors take heed!

Unlike the other nature reserves, this is largely farmland; of the 120 square kilometres, only nine are classified as natural reserve. The regulations are therefore less strict; apart from Olot there are places within the park like **Santa Pau** with hotel accommodation, and parking and camping are permitted in specified areas.

Some seventy-five per cent of the park is wooded, and the acidic volcanic soil particularly suits different varieties of oak. There are also fresh and leafy beech woods such as the famous Fageda de Jordà near Santa Pau, and plantations of alder in humid areas. Deer and wolves are now extinct, but wild boar are on the increase, and red squirrel, badgers, martens and mountain cats (*Felis sylvestris*), dying out elsewhere, are frequently to be found in the woods. No less than 143 species of birds have been observed in the park, among others the eagle (*Circaetus gallicus*), goshawk, peregrine falcon, woodpecker, tawny owl, nuthatch, wryneck and coal tit.

Freser-Setcases

The hunting reserve of the Núria Valley and Freser-Setcases north of Ribes de Freser (*see* p.77) extends to 202 square kilometres in the mountains bordering the French frontier. The Núria Valley was formerly an important summer pasturage for hundreds of thousands of sheep driven up from the lowlands, and the area was designated a reserve in 1966 to preserve the chamois, then in danger of extinction. Other species have since benefited and the reserve is particularly rich in bird life, which includes the golden eagle; Bonelli's eagle; the short-toed eagle which in summer preys on the vipers and whip snakes (*Coluber viridiflavus*) common in the Pyrenees; ptarmigan (and vultures which feed on them) and the snow finch.

THE NORTH

Girona (Gerona), half-way between the French frontier and Barcelona, lies on the route of visitors driving south, as in the past it formed the first defence against invaders from the north. Because of its strategic position on a small hill overlooking the junction of the Rivers Ter and Onyar, it has been much fought over. It several times changed hands during the Moorish period; its epic defence in 1285 by Pere (Peter) II was the undoing of Philip III of France and his ill-starred crusade (*see* p.24); and it was three times — twice unsuccessfully — besieged by the French during the Peninsular War. The third siege, lasting from May to December 1808, was one of the most stubbornly contested of the whole campaign. When, towards its end, an officer suggested retreat to the Spanish commander, Mariano Alvarez de Castro, then prostrated with dysentery, he snapped 'to the cemetery'. To another officer who complained of the lack of supplies, he retorted, 'When the last food is gone we will start eating the cowards, beginning with you.'

The old city is divided from the new by the River Onyar, with a rampart of tenements in shades of yellow and ochre reflected in the mirror of its water. The cathedral on high ground at the centre is surrounded by a network of narrow alleys, some cobbled and with flights of steps, steep canyons splashed with sunlight and inky shadows, others wider and with arcades housing shops, bars and restaurants. Facing a small square flanked by tall houses, the cathedral, begun in 1312, stands above a splendid flight of ninety-six steps. Its nave, immensely wide and high with fine Catalan barrel vaulting, is both imposing and moving in its simplicity. The chapter house museum contains fine fourteenth- and fifteenth-century gold and silverwork, a beautifully illuminated commentary on the Apocalypse of 975 and an entirely unique tapestry of the Creation dating from c.1100.

Near the cathedral are two other fine churches, the Gothic Sant Feliu built on foundations from which Roman sarcophagi were excavated, and Sant Pere de Galligants, a fortified Romanesque church of the twelfth century partly built into the city wall and housing an archaeological museum. The city's Museum of Art is in the Bishop's Palace adjacent to the cathedral, and is particularly interesting for its collection of Romanesque decorative work. Richard Ford relates a picturesque legend about the remains of Sant Narciso interred in the Church of Sant Feliu:

> When Philip le Hardi [Philip III of France], anxious to avenge the Sicilian Vespers, invaded Catalonia and began by appropriating the silver on the saint's tomb, there forthwith issued from the body a plague of flies: the authorities differ as to the colour, some affirming that they were white, others that they were tri-coloured, blue, green and red ... Be this as it may, these blue-bottles destroyed no less than 24,000 horse and 40,000 Frenchmen; nay, the king himself sickened and died at Perpiñan Oct. 5, 1285.

The Arab Baths, in a square behind the cathedral, in fact date from the end of the twelfth century, long after the Moors had left the region. With their horseshoe arches, they are, however, very much in the Mozarabic style and comprise an entry hall; a *frigidarium* or cold room with niches for hanging up clothes and an elegant eight-columned lantern above the pool; a *tepidarium* or hall for warm baths; and a *caldarium* or steam bath. Opposite the baths, flights of steps lead up to gardens

and the old walls, from which there are views across the city and the leafy Davesa park on the outskirts with its groves of tall plane trees.

Figueres, 37 km north of Girona along the *autopista*, is a bustling market town, best-known to visitors for Salvador Dalí; it was here that he was born and died. The Museo Dalí in the former Teatre Municipal was started and arranged by the maestro himself and attracts long queues all summer (if you tire of waiting, Figueres has two of the best restaurants in Catalonia in the Hotel-Restaurant Ampurdán and the Hotel Durán). A pleasant excursion east from Girona is to Banyoles, a small resort town set back from the tree-fringed Lake of Banyoles with its pleasure boats, lakeside cafés and restaurants, the venue for the rowing events of the 1992 Olympics. A few kilometres along the western side of the lake, shaded by great yew trees, stands the honey-coloured Romanesque church of Porqueres, one of the most perfect of its kind with its slim bell tower. Beyond Banyoles the C150 leads to Olot and the Garrotxa Volcanic Park (*see* p.85), first passing through Besalú. This small and picturesque town, approached by a fortified bridge over the River Fluvia, was the seat of the Counts of Besalú from the tenth to twelfth centuries, and with its Romanesque Church de Sant Pere, its old streets and houses and Jewish baths, preserves much of its medieval character.

Taking the Waters

Catalans have been taking the waters since Roman times and there are hot springs and springs of sparkling and mineral waters from Caldes de Boí in the Pyrenees to Vallfogona de Riucorb in the province of Tarragona. The virtues of the hot springs, rich in minerals, were well known to the Romans, who called them *aquae calidae* – hence the Catalan name *Caldes*. They are thickest on the ground rather south of Girona. One of the largest is Caldes de Malavella off the N11 to Barcelona, source of the famous Vichy Catalan, the first Catalan mineral water to be bottled and so-called because with its content of sodium bicarbonate, together with salts of lithium and fluorine, it is very similar in composition to the French Vichy water. There are two elaborate spa hotels in Caldes de Malavella with their own thermal springs, the Balneari Vichy Catalá and the Balneari Prats. Both offer hydrotherapy and other health treatments and facilities as well as extensive gardens, swimming pools and sophisticated restaurants. The Vichy Catalá was built in 1898 in neo-Moorish style by one of the exponents of Modernism, the architect Gaietà Buïgas.

Further south, near Granollers, Caldes de Montbui, where

OPPOSITE
In the cathedral precinct, Girona

the waters are the hottest in the Iberian Peninsula, surfacing at above 70°C, is the oldest of Catalonia's spas, mentioned by Pliny and Ptolemy (a Roman milestone survives at Can Vendrell nearby). The Roman pool, restored and kept in repair, was in service until 1350, when the domed roof fell in. By the nineteenth century Montbui was each year attracting three or four thousand bathers from all over Spain. Today, there are a number of establishments in the town: one of them, the small family-run Balneari Termes Solà has traditionally attracted painters and possesses quite a gallery, including brightly coloured canvases of the garden by the celebrated Joquim Mir.

Nearer Girona and to the south-east are the spas of Santa Coloma de Farners and Sant Hilari Sacalm. **Santa Coloma de Farners**, now a smiling and prosperous little market town, was the scene of one of the bloodiest episodes of the War of the Harvesters (*see* p.27), when in June 1640 an arrogant and drunken *agutzil* (government official) provoked a riot by attempting to billet troops on the town. He took refuge with his servants in the inn, which was surrounded and burnt down. As a reprisal the Madrid authorities razed the town to the ground, and this resulted in the descent of thousands of armed peasants on Barcelona and the murder of the Viceroy.

The hot springs of Termes Orion are 2 km outside the town and during the nineteenth century the water was used in the local hemp industry to soften the tough fibres. They became known for their medicinal properties at the time of the Carlist Wars when many of the wounded were treated and cured. The spa of Termes Orion, approached by a grand avenue of plane trees, dates from the nineteenth century and the grand staircase, the original elevator and the theatre are 'Noucentisme', a style in vogue between Modernism and Art Deco.

Sant Hilari Sacalm, 22 km from Santa Coloma by the GE551, is surrounded by springs. In the town itself the popular Font Vella water is bottled commercially, while you can drink it or fill your own jug at the Font de Ferro.

Sant Hilari is on the northern fringe of the **Serra de Montseny**, a beautiful and well-wooded range of mountains, with the peaks of Matagalls (1700 m, 5576 ft) and Turo de l'Home (1712 m, 5615 ft) near the centre and extending almost to Granollers in the south. A designated Natural Park covers some 310 square kilometres of the area. Thanks to the abundant rainfall, streams and springs abound and the vegetation in the valleys is luxuriant. From Sant Hilari a picturesque route through the mountains is by the GE520 to **Arbúcies** and then the GE543, GE520 and B520 via **Viladrau** (the source of yet another bottled water) to Vic. The road, little more than a track at times, first spirals through forests of beech, chestnut and cork oak, finally emerging on to high open ground, fragrant with wild thyme, bright with yellow broom in the spring, broken by dark clumps of pine and circled by mountains. If the time is right, it is worth stopping for lunch a few kilometres beyond Arbúcies at Les Pipes, a rustic restaurant and former water mill over the stream from the road and half hidden in the trees. The up-and-down floor, the old shafting and belts, a pot-bellied stove burning logs, and forthcoming black waiter from the deep south of the USA — not to mention trout just caught from the stream — make it the most individual of hostelries. Tracks and footpaths criss-cross the area, which is a hiker's paradise; information may be obtained from local tourist offices, and the Centre d'Excursionista de Catalunya at Carrer Paradis 10, off the Plaça Sant Jaume in Barcelona, which provides refuges in mountain areas with simple accommodation and cooking facilities, has the most extensive library of large-scale maps and guidebooks. These may also be obtained from bookshops in Barcelona such as the Libreria Catalonia in the Ronda de Sant Pere off the Plaça de Catalunya.

Arbúcies and the Serra de Montseny may be approached more directly from Barcelona by the A7 *autopista* and **Hostal-ric**, a village stretching endlessly uphill along a single street, but worth seeing for the enormous castle at the top (on my first visit I remember pausing for refreshment at a *taverna* and never reaching it!), which for long held out against Napoleon's army during the Peninsular War.

Vic (Vich) to the north-east of the Serra de Montseny and on the N152 from Barcelona to Puigcerdà and the French border, is a sizeable commercial town with manufactories of leather and textiles and famous for its salami-like *salchichón* (*see* p.188). Its fine cathedral was constructed in neo-classical style between 1781 and 1803 around a twelfth-century church built by the Abbot Oliba, of which only the tower remains. The interior was decorated in 1930 by the celebrated Catalan artist, Josep Maria Sert. His paintings were destroyed by fire during the Civil War, after which he set to work for a second time, but died before completing a magnificent series of huge frescoes with subjects such as the Original Sin, the Martyrdom of the Apostles and Injustice during the life of Jesus and in the history of Catalonia, painted with fire and passion. The excellent Museu Episcopal contains art of a different order with an exceptionally fine collection of Romanesque and Gothic carvings and paintings from churches in the neighbourhood.

The **Parador of Vic** is some fourteen kilometres outside the town in the Guillera mountains. A modern building in traditional style, it is built above the Embalse de Sau with long views across the lake and its encircling heights, an ideal place for an unhurried few days' break. There are numbers of attractive stone-built villages and old *masias* (farmhouses) some of them rather grand with their arcaded upper floor, in the area. **Rupit**, on the C153 north of Vic, is something of a show village and some of its houses have been reproduced for the Poble Espanyol in Barcelona. At the bottom of a steep, wooded valley, its grey stone houses with red-tiled roofs flank a narrow, winding street – though prepared for tourists and somewhat self-conscious, it is not yet spoilt.

Across country from Vic to the west and more easily approached from Barcelona via Manresa is **Cardona** with its great ochre castle, now one of the most palatial of Paradors. Massively walled and turreted, it dominates the small town, frowning down on spoil heaps and fertiliser plants, the twentieth century's ugly contribution to the landscape, half of them already abandoned and rusting away. A hill with strata of rock salt looking like snow out of season, rises directly opposite.

The castle was first built by the Carolingian Louis the Pious as a strongpoint to secure territories wrested from the Moors and about a century later was extended and strengthened by Guifré el Pilós. The Dukes of Cardona are descended from Ramon Folch, a nephew of the Emperor Charlemagne. Such was its strength that the castle remained impregnable for centuries: in 1711, during the War of the Spanish Succession, it was unsuccessfully stormed by French and Spanish troops; and at the time of the Peninsular War, General Lacy successfully defended it against Marshal Suchet in 1811. In the ensuing civil war it held out against repeated attacks by the Carlists.

During reconstruction the eleventh-century Church of Sant Vicenç within the fortified precinct was carefully restored. Inside, it is one of the most atmospheric of Paradors with its endless stone passages and stairs, and four-poster beds in the larger rooms. What has been added, like the baronial dining hall, with its great arched roof supports and massive window embrasures, has been built of stone and in period style.

Twenty kilometres to the west of Cardona by the C149, **Solsona** preserves part of its medieval fortifications: a moat, gateways and towers. The castle ruins rise above the old houses and narrow streets and it is here at Corpus Christi that young people in traditional costume dance to the rhythm of gun shots and there are processions of *gegants* (giants) accompanied by grotesque *capgrosses* in papier-maché headpieces. Little remains of the Romanesque cathedral apart from its three apses; the

arched and vaulted naves are Gothic and the façade Baroque. The Romanesque statue of the Virgen del Claustro is outstanding in the delicacy of the carving.

Courtyard in the Castle of Cardona

There is a quartet of large industrial towns to the north of Barcelona: Manresa, Terrassa, Sabadell and Granollers. **Sabadell** and **Terrassa** have been important centres for the manufacture of textiles since the nineteenth century and both possess interesting groups of Art Nouveau buildings. **Granollers** also has its buildings in the Modernistic style, and a fine Renaissance arcade, La Porxada, in the market square. **Manresa**, one of the places which put up the fiercest resistance to the French during the Peninsular War, was as a reprisal more or less razed to the ground by Marshal MacDonald in 1811.

The grotto of Santa Cova (now a chapel), where Ignacio Loyola spent a year in penance, commands a glorious view of the jagged profile of Monstserrat where he was to lay his sword on the altar of the monastery and dedicate himself to the foundation of the Society of Jesus (the Jesuits).

The holy mountain of **Montserrat** (Mons Serratus) is, in the words of Richard Ford, as 'jagged as a saw', and 'the outline is most fantastic, consisting of cones, pyramids, buttresses, nine pins, sugar loaves, which are here jumbled by nature in sportive mood.' Within less than an hour's drive from Barcelona by the new *autopista* to Terrassa it is a magnet for tourists for whom huge restaurants and other facilities have been created. The mountain against the side of which the monastery crouches rises abruptly to 1241 m (4072 ft) and access is either by a steeply spiralling road or cable railway. More impressive than the buildings with their severe horizontal lines, built to replace those laid waste by Marshal Suchet's troops in 1811 and then left to decay until the return of the monks in 1874, is the sublime setting. With small hermitages perched among the wooded crags (reached by cable car and mountain paths) and the long views towards Manresa and the mountains of the north and across the coloured patchwork of vineyards in the Penedès to the south, it is said that the great rocks of Montserrat inspired Wagner's setting for *Parsifal*.

The monastery owes its foundation to the discovery of a wooden image of the Virgin. According to legend, it was made by St Luke and brought to Barcelona in AD 50 by St Peter. It was hidden away on the hill from the invading Moors and rediscovered in 880 by shepherds attracted by heavenly lights and singing angels. The Bishop of Vic came in person and was guided by a sweet smell to the Santa Cova (Holy Cave), from which the Virgin refused to be moved. A shrine and chapel were therefore built on the spot. Later, a nunnery was founded and this was converted in 976 into a Benedictine monastery the present basilica dates from the sixteenth century and a new façade was added in 1900. The legend is markedly similar to that of the discovery of the Virgin of Guadalupe. Both figures are of dark wood, blackened by the kisses of countless pilgrims and the Montserrat figurine would seem to date from the twelfth century. She is now protected by a crystal niche above the high altar of the basilica, where twice daily services for the pilgrims, accompanied by beautifully sung Gregorian chants are celebrated at 11.00 and 18.45. The choir school, the Escalonia, founded in the twelfth century is one of the oldest in the world, and the Salve Regina is exquisitely sung at 13.00 and 19.00 on weekdays and at Mass on Sundays at 11.00.

Montserrat, more than a monastery, is a symbol of Catalan independence. During the Peninsular War it was fortified by the guerilla leader Eroles and, in Ford's words, 'being a natural citadel it was made a mountain magazine.' The loss of the 'Holy Hill' to the French – as a result of treachery according to Eroles – was as much a moral as tactical set-back, since, in Ford's words, the Catalans believed that 'their Queen of Heaven had deserted them, surrendered to the French.'

In the dark days after the Civil War, when even the Catalan language had been suppressed, some of the young priests began conducting the litany and Mass in Catalan. They received little support from the ecclesiastical hierarchy; Aureli Maria Escarré, Abbot of Montserrat, was an honourable exception. In 1963 he wrote in *La Monde*, 'The real subversion existing in Spain is that of the government of Spain.' At the prompting of the Vatican he was subsequently forced to resign.

Perhaps the most lyrical view of Montserrat is from the

View from Montserrat across the Penedès

Penedès in springtime, when the fields are sheets of red poppies and the turrets and pinnacles of the 'Holy Mountain' lie blue and mysterious on the horizon.

THE WEST AND SOUTH-WEST

The biggest city in the west of Catalonia and capital of its largest province is **Lleida** (Lérida). It lies on the River Segre at the centre of the largest stretch of arable land in the country watered by the Segre and Noguera rivers and the Urgell and Aragó canals. The wide plain grows apples, peaches, almonds and cereals; the oil from its olive groves is of such quality as to be demarcated; and the wines from Raimat (*see* p.172) are among the best from Spain. Around Lleida, each town has its agricultural cooperative or plant for packing, canning, bottling or processing fruit or vegetables.

As a centre of communications Lleida has been much fought over and has suffered more sieges and massacres than any other city in Catalonia. It was here that Julius Caesar out-generalled and defeated the forces of his rival, Pompey (the fine stone bridge across the Segre is built on Roman foundations). Guifré el Pilós, founder of the House of Barcelona, died as the result of a mortal wound received at the hands of its Moorish governor, Lope ibn-Muhammad. The city was besieged and cruelly sacked during the War of the Spanish Succession, and the French again outdid themselves at the time of the Peninsular War when the women and children were driven out of the town and exposed to murderous fire from Suchet's artillery brought to an end only when the Spanish governor ran up the white flag on the citadel to spare further slaughter of the innocent. Commenting on this, Suchet's apologist, General Foy, eulogizes 'the sublime revelations of the genius of destruction, which evoke powers of thought far superior to those giving birth to poetry or philosophy.' Such parts of old Lleida which survived were largely razed during the Spanish Civil War.

Lleida therefore has more than its share of modern streets and often ugly commercial and apartment buildings. On a hill in the middle stands the skeleton of the ravaged thirteenth century cathedral, with its gaunt octagonal tower. Richard Ford, with more than a touch of malice, reports that 'in the piping times of peace the steep walk proved too much for the stall-fed canons, whose affections were not set on things above: so they abandoned the lofty church ...' The truth seems to be that after the siege of Lleida in 1707 it was converted into a barracks by Philip V, the first of the Spanish Bourbons, a art of the reprisals for Catalonia's siding against him in the War of the Spanish Succession. Only the beautiful Gothic loister with long views over the Segre evokes the cathedral's ast glories. The Catedral Nova (New Cathedral) is an unin-piring neo-classical structure; opposite it the fifteenth-century Hospital de Santa Maria has a fine arcaded patio and houses an rchaeological museum with important Roman and pre-Roman ollections.

Cervera, about half-way between Lleida and Barcelona on he N11, also has its associations with Philip V. It was here, fter he had banned the use of Catalan, either spoken or in ooks, and closed the University of Barcelona, that he built a ew university in 1716. The university has long since been bandoned, but the building, later gutted by Suchet to make a arracks, remains. Apart from this, a renegade Spaniard, as ord relates, 'placed all his countrymen who did not pay French ontributions into a cage, leaving outside their heads be-meared with honey to attract a plague of flies.' He later met is just deserts at the hands of the Catalan guerrillas. Cervera as kept some of its medieval houses and it was in one of them hat the Generalitat was first established in 1359. The town all is an interesting eighteenth-century building with a bal-ony supported by caryatids.

THE GREAT MONASTERIES

n the area between Lleida and Tarragona there are four great monasteries, the Cistercian foundations of Poblet, Santes Creus nd Vallbona de les Monges, and the Carthusian Scala Dei. All uffered extensive damage in the wake of the first Carlist War, vhen the peasants took the opportunity to settle scores with he Church. Many of them loathed and feared the feudal owers of the monks (which not so long before included rights o the bridal night of their female serfs), at the same time oveting their great estates. An orgy of destruction followed. And when the liberal President of the *Consejo de Ministros*, Alvarez Mendizábal, introduced the Royal Decrees of February nd March 1836 disentailing the religious orders and appropri-ting their property for the state, it sealed the fate of many eligious establishments. In one form or another the three Cistercian monasteries weathered the storm; Scala Dei remains n overgrown ruin.

Vallbona de les Monges may be approached either from Tarrega to the north on the N11 or from Prats on the A2 *utopista* to the south. Dating from 1157, it is the smallest of he four and is served by Cistercian nuns. The style, as with

Picnickers by the Lake of Banyoles

Poblet and Santes Creus, is a transition from Romanesque to Gothic, with a large cloistered patio flanked by the church, chapter house and other dependencies. The lantern tower of the church is particularly fine.

The simplest way to Poblet, in the hilly wine-growing area of the Conca de Barberà, is by the N240 from Tarragona via **Valls** and **Montblanc**. Valls is best known for its *calçotadas*, a mass celebration of the spring onion (*see* p.209) and for teams of athletic young men in traditional costume competing to form human towers or *castells*. The season begins on the feast of Sant Joan (24 June). Montblanc was one of the most important towns of Catalonia in medieval times, and meetings of the *Corts* (parliament) were held here on several occasions. Its fourteenth-century walls with their high towers survive, as also the fourteenth-century Church of Santa Maria, the Romanesque Sant Miquel, a Gothic bridge and baronial houses.

Poblet is just off the N240 at L'Espluga de Francolí. The huge monastery, once more of a fortified town than house of God – with its hostels, granaries, stables, vineyards and wine cellars, orchards and gardens – was founded in 1151 by Ramon Berenguer IV and was the burial place of the rulers of the Crown of Aragon from the time of Pere III (1336–87). More than that, many of the Catalan monarchs spent their last years there, the abbot acting much as a royal chaplain. As Ford remarked, 'this is truly characteristic of the mediaeval Spaniard, half soldier, half monk, a crusading knight of Santiago, his manhood spent in combating for the cross, his declining years dedicated to religion.' In fact, some of the sepulchres have two effigies, one representing the king as a soldier, and the other as a monk.

The monastery was plundered by the French during the Peninsular War and then completely wrecked and looted by the anti-clerical peasantry during the riots of 1835. The utter destruction was vividly evoked by Augustus Hare, writing in 1873:

> It is the very abomination of desolation ... the most utterly ruined ruin that can exist. Violence and vengeance are written on every stone. The vast walls, the mighty courts, the endless cloisters, look as if the shock of a terrible earthquake had passed over them. There is no soothing vegetation, no ivy, no flowers ... Caryatides without arms or faces, floating angels wingless and headless, flowers without stems and leaves without branches, all dust-laden, cracked and crumbling ...

Restoration began a century later in 1940; the monks have returned; the royal remains, rescued during the desecration of

the church, have been reinterred and their tombs reconstructed; and tranquillity restored to the lofty church with its great curtain wall and towers.

The Cistercian monastery of Poblet

Santes Creus lies a few kilometres from Exit 11 (for Valls) of the A2 *autopista*, but on the northern side of the road. It is often described as the rival of Poblet, since both date from the same period in the twelfth century, are built in the same mixture of Romanesque and Gothic and enjoyed the special protection of the Catalan kings and nobility. Two of the kings chose to be buried here: Pere II ('The Great') and near him his admiral, the great Roger de Llúria; and Jaume II (1291–1327) who lies with his wife, Blanche of Anjou. One of the glories of Santes Creus is the cloister with its beautiful Gothic tracery, designed in part by the English architect Reinard Fonoll between 1332 and 1336, enclosing topiary hedges and borders of roses, with the golden stone of its church and lantern tower rising behind.

The Monastery of **Scala Dei**, the mother house of almost all the Carthusian monasteries in Spain and Portugal, is sadly another story. In the mountains of the Serra de Montsant some 25 km beyond Reus by the C242, it lies behind the village of Scala Dei, a cluster of stone houses at the bottom of a natural

OVERLEAF LEFT
The castle of the Duques de Cardona, now a Parador

OVERLEAF RIGHT
Street in the village of Rupit

101

Carthaginian and Roman amphoras in the Museu de Vi in Vilafranca del Penedès

amphitheatre and the centre of the wine district (*see* p.171) of El Priorat (Priorato) named in reference to the monastery. It was founded in 1162 by Alfons II, as the legend goes on a spot where the countryfolk had seen angels ascending and descending a ladder into the heavens. What remains of the once magnificent buildings are gateways and walls overgrown with creeper, a great church in red stone, roofless and with trees thrusting up inside the nave, and the vestiges of two grand cloisters with the monks' cells giving off them. Outside the main precinct are a ruined chapel and hermitage, and buildings once used as a retreat by the Catalan clergy. What was saved from the great library is now in the Seminary in Tarragona.

WINE TOWNS OF THE PENEDÈS

The capital of the wine-growing *comarca* (county) of the Penedès (*see also* pp.163–4) lying south-west of Barcelona and Montserrat is **Vilafranca del Penedès**, surrounded by vineyards, off the A7 *autopista* from Barcelona to Tarragona. Founded by Hamilcar Barca, it is said to be the earliest Carthaginian settlement in Catalonia and after it was retaken from the Moors *c.*1000 it was named a 'free town' – hence the name – and given special privileges so as to attract settlers to the disturbed frontier region. It is a pleasant country town, with a tree-fringed square at the centre, good restaurants and with wineries clustered around the railway station. The largest, Bodegas Torres, with its great wooden vats and interesting display of old wine presses, is open to visitors (*see* p.165).

The Museu del Vi (Wine Museum) is one of the best in or outside Spain. It is housed in a former palace of the Kings of Aragon-Catalonia, which they donated to the Monastery of Santes Creus when they built a new palace in the fourteenth century beside the Church of Santa Maria opposite. The displays begin with Greek, Carthaginian and Roman amphorae and tableaux representing wine-making from Egyptian times onwards. They continue with examples of old agricultural and wine-making equipment – ploughs, presses, barrels, corking devices and the rest, of different periods from the very ancient. There are also extensive exhibits of bottles, glassware and *porrones* of every size and shape, and of decorative tiles and paintings relating to wine. The visit ends in a small bar, where a representative range of Penedès wines may be tasted.

The town possesses the oldest *drac* (dragon) in Catalonia, paraded around the streets during the festivities on St George's day (*see* p.54), though it seems that after hospitalization he is to be placed in the local museum and a plastic replica is to take his place on the streets.

Vilafranca makes still wines and liqueurs; the other important wine town, **Sant Sadurní d'Anoia**, is the headquarters of *cava* and the sparkling wine industry (*see* p.149). A pleasant twenty-minute drive from Vilafranca by the C243 through rolling vineyard country, it may also be approached direct by the A7 *autopista* from Barcelona. Known as Noela to Pliny (hence the name Anoia), it is claimed to have been founded by Noah, whose ark appears on its escutcheon. Be this as it may, in its sixty or so *cavas* (wineries) it certainly makes enough sparkling wine to float the ark, although the evidences of this are mainly in the miles of cellars below ground. On the surface it is a little town centering on a winding main street, without a hotel or much in the way of a restaurant, with the two most impressive, and indeed vast, wineries of Codorníu and Freixenet on the edge.

Both of these establishments welcome visitors, and the visit to Codorníu with its decorative gardens, the train ride around its 18 km of underground cellars, and the wine museum in the lofty stone-vaulted building of the old press house is especially interesting. These and some of the other wineries, like that of Segura Viudas, with the blue heights of Montserrat rising behind it, are described in Chapter IV.

Drinking from a *porró* at the Museu de Vi in Vilafranca del Penedès

THE EBRE (EBRO) VALLEY

The Ebro, as it is generally known, enters Catalonia west of El Priorat, where it then becomes the Ebre, and with a great sweep eastwards, the scene of one of the fiercest battles of the Civil War, descends through some of the most beautiful mountain country in Catalonia to its delta beyond Tortosa.

The Battle of the Ebro was a desperate counterattack by the Republicans on Franco's army deployed to the west of the Ebre in the Terra Alta. On the night of 24/25 July 1938, the advance guard of some 100,000 Republican troops achieved complete surprise by crossing the river at Flix, Móra la Nova and Miraset. The Nationalists succeeded in fighting off an attack on the key town of Gandesa, and during the war of attrition that followed every yard of ground was contested during a suffocating summer and until the first snows of winter, when the Republicans finally retreated across the river. One of the last to cross was Ernest Hemingway. Casualties were appalling, with some 70,000, including 30,000 dead on the Republican side, and upwards of 30,000 Nationalists.

Today, driving along the winding country roads, bordered by peach and cherry orchards, almond and olive groves, and vineyards, ringed by blue mountains on the horizon, it is

OVERLEAF
El Masroig, near Mora la Nova

105

hard to believe that this peaceful landscape saw some of the bloodiest fighting of the twentieth century. One may follow the valley down by taking the N230 from the industrial centre of Flix and crossing the river at Asco, the site of an atomic power station, to join the C230 to Móra la Nova. Here, there is a bridge across the river, and the N420 passes isolated hilltop townships like El Masroig, a cluster of white houses crowned by a mosque turned church, before crossing the mountains to the east and descending by a spectacular corniche to Reus. In the other direction it is 24 km to Gandesa; largely flattened during the Civil War, it has been rebuilt, but possesses a wine cooperative built in Modernist style in 1919 by the architect Cèsar Martinell, and is the centre of the wine trade in the demarcated region of the Terra Alta. A few kilometres to its west, the shattered village of Corbrera d'Ebre stands as the shells and bombs left it, a memorial to those who died.

From Móra la Nova, one may either take the C230 running close to the Ebre before joining the N230 for Tortosa north of Xerta, or alternatively the enchanting T324, a narrow byroad weaving its erratic way between orchards, olive groves and vineyards and eventually joining the N230 further north. This route has the advantage of passing through the fascinating little towns of Miravet and El Pinell de Brai (it is easy to see why Picasso spent a couple of summers at Horta de Sant Joan further west, since every turn of the road and new view of the green and ochre landscape suggests a painting). Miravet, a quiet place of white houses, is dominated by the bulk of the Knights Templars' castle, set on the hillside with its rectangular curtain walls like a great stone drawer. It may be reached by river boat from Amposta (see p.125) and there is also a paddle ferry from the opposite bank, and attracts tourists because of its artesan potteries, making and selling stoneware very much in the Moorish tradition. El Pinell de Brai, near the junction with the N230, is another picturebook township and stands on a hillock islanded in vineyards.

Tortosa, near the mouth of the Ebre and its delta, is the largest town in the region, and because of its strategic position has been increasingly fought over down the centuries. The Roman Dertosa Julia Augusta was founded by the Scipios on the site of the Iberian Hibera. The city was captured by the Moors in 714, who built the Castle of La Zuda above it, now the site of the modern Parador. It remained in Moorish hands for almost three centuries until it was taken by Ramon Berenguer IV with the help of the Knights Templars and Genoese, and would have fallen to them again but for the heroism of its women. The story goes that they manned the

El Pinell de Brai in the high valley of the Ebro

battlements while their men sallied out against the Moors and that the grateful Ramon Berenguer awarded them the Order of the Axe and the right to take precedence over men at official ceremonies. The last and most devastating of its sieges took place during the Civil War and Battle of the Ebro, as a result of which much of the town apart from the area around the cathedral was destroyed. A memorial to the fallen stands in the middle of the river.

The cathedral was begun in 1347 and is built in elegant Gothic, though the classical façade added in the eighteenth century has often been criticized for being out of character. Rose Macaulay vigorously contests this: 'The Tortosa façade has beauty, dignity and grace, and goes piquantly with the flying buttresses and russet-tiled roofs of the battlemented building.' Most would agree with her in thinking the thirteenth-century cloister with its slender columns and pointed arches, rather than the exuberant Baroque of the Chapel of Nuestra Señora de la Cinta, the jewel of the cathedral. Apart from the cathedral the fine fourteenth-century Episcopal Palace with its beautiful courtyard and the Llotja, a covered market hall of the same period, survived the bombardment of the Civil War.

Tortosa is a pleasant town with good shops, and its Parador, with the winding, uphill approach through the outworks of the old fortress, is spacious and comfortable and has a good

The Roman aqueduct at Tarragona

OPPOSITE
Romanesque church at Porqueres

restaurant. Little of the original castle remains, and it is one of the most elaborate exercises in period reconstruction undertaken by an organization which (as at Jaén) specializes in this. The grounds are extensive and there are magnificent views up and down the Ebre and over the roofs of the city from their battlements.

THE COSTA DAURADA

The Costa Daurada (Costa Dorada) with its sunshine and fine golden sand extends from Barcelona to the Ebro delta (Delta de L'Ebre) and has become one of the most popular stretches of the Spanish Mediterranean with holiday-makers.

After passing Barcelona airport, the dual carriageway of the C246 runs through pine woods and camping sites alive with people and cars from Barcelona at summer weekends. The first town, **Castelldefels**, is a prime favourite of the Barceloneses during the season and has a good beach and restaurants and shops galore. Beyond Castelldefels the road narrows and climbs to the top of the cliffs in a series of sweeping curves. For the next 16 km the views across the sea are splendid, spoilt only by one of the largest cement works in Spain, with its quarries, conveyer belts and jetties incongruously sited alongside the road.

At **Aiguadolç**, just off the main road before entering Sitges, there is an impressive new marina with cheerful restaurants and bars just across from the yacht basin. It was at Aiguadolç that Malvasia vines brought from Greece by a seaman from the fleet of Roger de Llúria were first planted (*see* p.143). **Sitges**, the Subur of the Romans, has survived its popularity as a tourist resort with grace. When still a small fishing town with its church looking down from a rocky promontory to the small beach of Sant Sebastiá, it was 'discovered' at the end of the nineteenth century by the artists Santiago Rusiñol and Miguel Utrillo, who, like Salvador Dalí at Cadaqués, attracted other artists and writers. Rusiñol left his house, Cau Ferrat, to the town, together with his collection. It is now a museum containing wrought iron, ceramics and glass; the drawings and paintings include works by Rusiñol, Miguel Utrillo, Ramon Casas and two canvases by El Greco. The artist community soon expanded, and it was not long before it became fashionable for well-to-do Catalans from Vilafranca, Barcelona and further afield to build summer residences in Sitges, and behind the sea front and old town a network of quiet streets, planted with pink and white oleander and acacia trees, are bordered by villas, nineteenth-century, Edwardian and modern, in large

The Costa Daurada

well-kept and well-watered gardens. The area comes to life in the summer and at weekends during the rest of the year with house parties arriving in Mercedes limousines, cocktails by the swimming pool and pretty girls in beach shorts zooming about on motor scooters.

Holiday activities centre on the wide beach, the Platja d'Or and palm-fringed esplanade, backed by elegant restaurants and boutiques. The axis of the old town is Parellades, a narrow street running uphill from the main square, the Plaça d'Espanya. Closed to traffic and shaded and cool in summer, it is a promenade for locals and holidaymakers alike and one may buy elegant clothes and shoes, provisions, wine, ironmongery or anything else. As elsewhere in Spain, the hairdressers are expert and highly to be recommended. At the top, along a turning to the right to the church is a *confiteria* worth visiting, apart from its patisserie, for the elegance of its decorations resembling something from Jane Austen's Bath. To the left and three turnings along in the Espalter, which also leads to the Plaça d'Espanya, is one of the very best *xarcuterias* (charcuteries) in Spain, selling *salchichón*, *jamón serrano*, and *chorizos* of every type, as well as cheeses from all over Spain.

Sitges is well-known for the festival at Corpus Christi; the *Festa major* at the end of August, celebrated with country dancing; and the harvest festival in September when wine flows free from a fountain on the esplanade, and the Queen of the Wine Harvest is driven in state to one of the churches for the blessing of the grapes. Just north of Sitges on the road to Vilafranca del Penedès, the village of **Sant Pere de Ribes** is said to have produced the best wine of the Penedès in the eighteenth century, 'dark, exquisite and with strength' as it was described at the time. A mansion on the outskirts houses the elegant Gran Casino de Barcelona with its gaming tables and de luxe restaurant.

A short distance down the coast from Sitges off the C246, **Vilanova i la Geltrú** is the third port in Catalonia, frequented by the Greeks and Phoenicians, which in the eighteenth century shipped large amounts of brandy and Penedès wines to London, Amsterdam, Russia and North America. Thanks to the cotton industry, developed in the eighteenth and nineteenth centuries, Vilanova is now largely industrial, but there are good beaches, comfortable hotels, and some excellent seafood restaurants serving the fish caught locally. Some of the old streets at the centre remain, and there are three excellent museums. The late eighteenth-century and early nineteenth-century Casa Papiol is furnished in period style with harbingers of Modernism, such as gas lighting, and contains the room in Louis XVI style used by Marshal Suchet during the Peninsular War, reception and music rooms, a billiard room, bedrooms with decorations in *grisaille*, a tiled kitchen with the original oven, a store for olive oil and other domestic amenities of the time. The thirteenth-century Castell de la Geltrú now houses a collection of modern Catalan painting.

There are numbers of coastal resorts between Vilanova i la Geltrú and Tarragona. Rose Macaulay recalls how she slept at 'the tiny fishing beach of Calafell' and that when her car got stuck in the sand it took the whole population to dig it out, adding that 'They had not, it seemed, had foreign visitors before at Calafell playa.' Today, **Calafell, El Vendrell** and **Torredembarra**, are all thriving summer resorts, especially frequented by the Germans and French. Like the other places along this coast, they are, incidentally, served by train from Barcelona, a much pleasanter way of reaching them at weekends than by the crowded coastal road (it can take a solid hour in nose-to-tail traffic to enter or leave Barcelona at peak periods either by the *autopista* or C246). Between Calafell and Torredembarra the road, the ancient Via Augusta running from the Pyrenees to Cartagena, divides around a Roman triumphal arch, the best of its kind in Spain, erected in the early years of the second century BC by Lucius Sergius Sura, one of Trajan's generals. **Altafulla**, an attractive town some 12 km from Tarragona, was a fashionable resort even in Roman times, and a large villa has been excavated here.

By the side of the road some 7 km from **Tarragona** is the so-called Tower of the Scipios, a worn grey Roman tomb supposed to contain the remains of Publius and Gnaeus Scipio defeated and killed by the Carthaginians in 211 BC. It was of the view from here that Richard Ford wrote his lyrical description of the city:

> The view towards Tarragona is ravishing: here the beauty of the present is heightened by the poetry of the past. The rock-built city slopes with its lines of wall down to the mole, which is studded with white sails; the vapoury distant hills and the blue sea peep through vistas of the red branches of the pines, and glitter through the dark velvet of their tufted heads ...

Tarragona was important in Iberian times before Publius and Gnaeus Cornelius Scipio joined forces there in 217 BC. Roman Tarraco subsequently became the capital of the northern province of Tarraconensis, the largest in Spain, and the second city of the Empire. With its balmy climate, its theatres, forum, games and chariot races, stag and boar hunting and mellow

OVERLEAF
Souvenir stalls, Ebro delta

wines, it soon became a residence of poets, writers, gastro-nomes and of the Emperors Augustus, Galba and Hadrian. It has preserved more of its Roman heritage than anywhere else in Spain apart, perhaps, from its sister city of Mérida, Roman capital of Lusitania in the west. It is said that it was here that St Paul made the first Spanish converts to Christianity, and the diocese is the premier in Spain. The destruction of Tarragona's Roman glories was begun by the Franks and Visigoths in the third century and completed by the Moors in the eighth.

As it stands today, the city is divided (like all Gaul) into three parts: the port to the south, in whose dusty streets the bodegas and wine shippers once stood side by side, but now largely dominated by an oil refinery and petrochemical installations; on the high ground above, the modern city; and crowning it, the old town with its great walls and cathedral.

Inside Tarragona, the chief Roman remains include the amphitheatre by the beach, where Bishop Fruitós was martyred in 258, and of which much remains; above it are the praetorium and the circus, currently being excavated. Much reconstructed in medieval times, the Praetorium was the residence of Augustus, and Pontius Pilate was born here while

Former Chartreuse distillery at Tarragona

his father was governor of Tarraconensis. The small portion of the Circus Maximus which has been unearthed hardly conveys an idea of racing charioteers and cheering spectators by the thousand, and underlines the difficulty of excavation in built-up areas, since the works stop short at a rampart of houses and without their demolition cannot continue. The great Roman walls, at least – the so-called Passeig Arqueologic – stand massively intact. It is thought that they were constructed by the Scipios on the basis of huge 'Cyclopean' blocks of stone piled on top of one another without cement. Today they are ringed by lawns and cypress trees, and inside are the Cathedral and the narrow streets of the old city. The Museu Arqueologic at the southern edge of the old city contains a fascinating collection of Roman artefacts, including statues and friezes which adorned the squares and public places, medallions from the Temple of Jupiter, and among other mosaics, a splendid head of Medusa. (Some of the most impressive Roman remains lie outside the city – *see* p.117 and below).

The great fortress-like cathedral, built of honey-coloured stone on the site of the Roman temple of Jupiter faces a flagged courtyard above a flight of steps at the end of the former Roman Via Triumphalis. It was begun in the twelfth century at a time when the Romanesque style was giving way to Gothic. Make your way as best you can in the prevailing darkness to the high altar, above which there is a finely detailed painting by the fourteenth-century Pere Johan. Among the glories of the cathedral are the airy, sun-filled Gothic cloisters, beautifully carved in Cistercian style and giving on to a wide patio planted with palms, oleander, oranges and roses, with the towers and nave soaring above.

The main thoroughfare of the modern city is the wide tree-lined Rambla Nova, lined by shops and open-air cafés, which proceeds straight as a die towards the sea, where it stops short at the Balcó Mediterrani, a viewpoint over the Mediterranean appropriately adorned with a statue of Roger de Llúria, the thirteenth-century admiral who ruled its waters. Tarragona possesses four clean and good beaches in or near the city: La Platja del Miracle, La Rabassada, La Sabinosa and La Platja Larga. What, surprisingly, we have never succeeded in finding is a good hotel, though El Sol Ric is one of the best restaurants in Catalonia.

The most remarkable of Tarragona's Roman remains, the Aqueduct (Aqueducte de les Farreres – so-called because of the rusty colour of the water) – is 4 km outside the town off the road to Valls. Extraordinarily, it is not even signposted, and access is by a spinney to the side of the road. Ten minutes

The ruined monastery of Scala Dei

Museu de Vi (Wine Museum) in Vilafranca del Penedès

Footpath along the top
of the Roman aqueduct,
Tarragona

scramble along a stony, shrub-grown path then reveals the magnificent aqueduct with its double tier of arches of golden stone riding the valley (it can also be seen, but not approached, on the left hand side of the A7 *autopista* travelling towards Barcelona). It is so perfectly preserved that one can walk along the channel at the top from one side of the valley to the other – though the parapet is low and this is not to be recommended to the vertiginous! Off a by-road to Reus at Centcelles near **Constanti**, there is another notable Roman survival in the form of a great mausoleum built by a wealthy landowner of the fourth century AD on his property. The first chamber, topped by a 9 m (30 ft) dome, contains mosaics with early Christian themes, such as Daniel and the lions, and the second, apses on either side.

Some ten kilometres south of Tarragona, **Salou** (and **Cambrils** just beyond it), with their teaming holiday beaches, the concrete ramparts of their hotels, the apartment blocks, and the palm- and bar-fringed esplanades are laid out for package tours. Charter flights from northern Europe fly direct to the bustling industrial town of **Reus**, 15 km inland of Tarragona, a centre of the wine trade and more recently for the hazelnuts grown on a huge scale in the surrounding area. (It was the birthplace of the famous architect Antoni Gaudí, but there is nothing to show apart from some Modernist façades by his contemporary Domènech y Montaner). To return to Cambrils, it is surprisingly quiet out of season and possesses three restaurants owned and run by various members of the Gatell family (*see* p.197), serving such excellent seafood that they are worth the drive from Tarragona or beyond. **Miami Platja** and **L'Hospitalet**, further south on what is now the N340, are custom-built holiday resorts with the obligatory high-rise apartments and supermarkets, but **L'Ametlla de Mar**, on a rockier stretch of coast further on, while catering for campers and yachtsmen, still has much of the feeling of a fishing village with its chandlers and open shed auctioning fish caught by local boats.

THE EBRO DELTA (DELTA DE L'EBRE)

The Ebro is one of the great rivers of Spain, rising in the mountains of Santander in the north and passing through the Rioja and Zaragoza before entering Catalonia, where it is known as the Ebre. Its delta, an area of marshland, rice fields and beaches, juts out into the Mediterranean like a parrot's beak, as Rose Macaulay aptly described it, for a distance of some 40 km. In the time of the Moors during the twelfth century the delta extended for only a few kilometres into the sea, and it seems that its huge extension took place largely in medieval times as a result of wholesale deforestation in the upper Ebro valley and the accumulation of alluvial silt at the mouth of the river.

Today, the delta, with the Ebre running through its centre, occupies a total area of some 350 square kilometres, of which 280 are paddy fields and orchards, with another 70 being devoted to the largest nature reserve in Catalonia.

A good centre for visiting both the northern and southern parts of the delta, with bridges across the river and also river boats plying upstream on a highly scenic route as far as Miravet (*see* p.108), is **Amposta**. Known as Ibera in ancient times, it was then the strongest town of the Ebre and as an ally of Carthage withstood all the assaults of the Scipios until Hasdrubal left Spain and was killed in Italy while attempting to reinforce his brother, Hannibal. Further south along the N340 is the old town of **Sant Carles de la Ràpita** on one of the largest natural anchorages in the Mediterranean, the Port dels Alfacs (from an Arabic word meaning 'delta'), which Carlos III dreamed of making a great port. His unfinished palace and other ruins remain, but the grandiose plan was abandoned on his death in 1788. A few kilometres beyond Sant Carles is **Les Cases d'Alcanar**, a small fishing village turned fashionable holiday place, on the border of the province of Castellón de la Plana and the Costa Blanca.

The large-scale agricultural development of the delta began with the construction of canals on both sides of the Ebre in the mid nineteenth century. At the time, malaria was a serious problem – there had been some 3000 deaths up to 1918 – but since 1857 the population has grown from 5278 to some 40,000, the largest town being the sizeable **Deltebre**, until recently known as **La Cava**, at the centre and on the north bank of the river. Driving towards it through the pancake-flat landscape in spring, the rice fields, flooded from May until October, mirror the sky and clouds, with white-walled, red-tiled farms and the small houses of the agricultural workers scattered alongside. The delta with its semi-tropical climate grows more rice than the famous Albufera of Valencia, the birthplace of *paella*, and apart from fruit also produces large amounts of fish and shellfish, especially prawns and lobsters, from ports such as L'Ampolla and Sant Carles de la Rápita. There is an information centre for the nature reserve at Deltebre, and driving on towards the mouth of the river one arrives at a landing stage for **Buda Island** on the opposite side of the river, one of the main conservation zones. By the quayside there are a couple of highly colourful open air

OPPOSITE
Rambla de les Flors,
Barcelona

RIGHT
Street in the Gothic
quarter of Barcelona

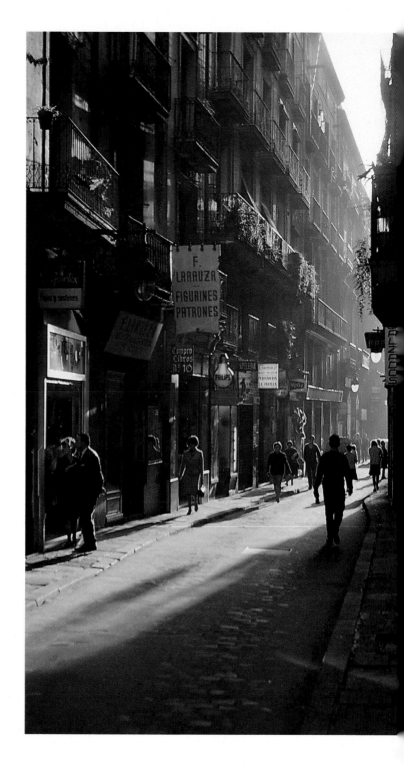

souvenir stands selling pottery and brightly coloured hats, flapping briskly in the breeze, and this is also the departure point for the large riverboats with their observation lounges heading downstream for worthwhile trips around the mouth of the river.

The Parc Natural del Delta de l'Ebre was designated a nature reserve in 1983 and apart from the Camargue in France is the most important of its kind in the western Mediterranean. In Spain, it is second in size only to the Coto Doñana on the Atlantic shores of the Gulf of Cádiz. The Park comprises separate areas of marshland, lagoons, sand bars and saltpans along the shores of the delta, and maps and brochures may be obtained at the information centres at Amposta, Sant Carles de la Ràpita, Deltebre and the Casa de Fusta on the Encanyissada lagoon. There are narrow roads in most parts of the delta, but cars are not allowed on Buda Island, nor is access to certain areas permitted during the breeding season.

The delta is above all interesting for its bird life. Its paddy fields provide a winter home for migratory birds from northern Europe, and north of the river in the Fangar peninsula jutting into the blue Gulf of Sant Jordi, terns, eider ducks and cormorants are regularly to be seen. The best starting point for a visit to the southern area is the Casa de Fusta information centre, where there is a raised hide with views over the large lagoon of L'Encanyissada. There are other hides on the nearby lagoon of La Tancada, where black and white avocets may frequently be seen, and overlooking the salt pans of the Punta de la Banya at the southern extremity of the delta. Because of its isolation and proximity to the feeding grounds of the sheltered Bay of Alfacs, this is the area richest of all in bird life. It is one of the few breeding grounds in Europe of the flamingo, and a large flight of the beautiful birds with their pinkish plumage and scarlet wing coverts is an unforgettable spectacle.

BARCELONA

Barcelona is the second city of Spain and the largest and most densely populated on the shores of the Mediterranean. Almost three quarters of Catalonia's population live in and around it, which perhaps explains why, abroad at any rate, the city is so much better known than the region of which it is the capital.

This was not so during its early history. It is sometimes said that it was first settled by the Carthaginians and that Hamilcar Barca gave it his own name of Barcino, but the city proper was founded by the Romans during the reign of Augustus (27 BC – AD 14) on the small hill at the centre of what is now called the

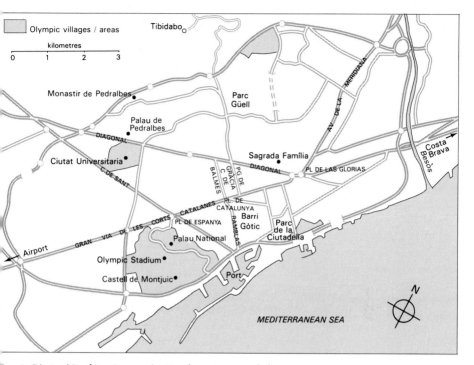

Map labels:
Olympic villages / areas
kilometres
0 1 2 3
Tibidabo
Monastir de Pedralbes
Parc Güell
Palau de Pedralbes
DIAGONAL
Ciutat Universitaria
C. DE SANT
PG DE GRÀCIA
C DE BALMES
Sagrada Família
DIAGONAL
PL DE LAS GLORIAS
Costa Brava
Besòs
PL. DE CATALUNYA
CORTS CATALANES
PL DE ESPANYA
RAMBLAS
Barri Gòtic
Parc de la Ciutadella
Airport
GRAN VIA DE LES CORTS CATALANES
Palau National
Olympic Stadium
Castell de Montjuic
Port
MEDITERRANEAN SEA
N

Plan of Barcelona

Barri Gòtic (Gothic Quarter). At that time and for centuries after it was a place of little consequence in comparison with the magnificent Tarragona, the Tarraco of the Romans, capital of the great northern province of Tarraconensis. By the time that it was occupied by the Moors in 717–19 it was already of some importance, and after its recapture by the Franks in 801 and the subsequent emergence of the Counts of Barcelona as the ruling dynasty it became recognized as the capital of the region. During the thirteenth and fourteenth centuries, when Catalan sea power dominated the Mediterranean, the port became of prime importance; and it was extended to its present size during the industrial boom of the nineteenth century, when the city itself expanded by leaps and bounds.

Barcelona lies between the sea to the south, the hills of Tibidabo and Vallvidrera to the north and Montjuïc to the west. There are two very definite parts: the old city and port area with narrow irregular streets, and the much larger Eixample, the rectangular grid of wide tree-lined avenues laid out in the late nineteenth century. Two great avenues, the Gran Via de les Corts Catalanes and the Avinguda de la Diagonal cut clean through the centre with direct access to *autopistas* on either side. Seen from Montjuïc above, the vast sea of buildings crowded into a hollow between the hills and sea conveys an impression of unbelievable concentration; on the ground,

129

thanks to its wide avenues and its parks, it often seems a spacious city. Certainly it possesses enormous and unmistak able personality, with its contrasts between old and new – the Gothic cathedral and Gaudí's unfinished Sagrada Família for a start; the open-air flower market and bookstalls of the Rambla with Columbus on his column at the lower end, beckoning towards the port and sea; the great museums and exhibition halls on Montjuïc; or the Modernistic houses and elegant shops of the Passeig de Gràcia.

In the old city, the best way to get about is to walk; along the main thoroughfares like the Diagonal and Gran Via the traffic roars and snarls a dozen abreast and on the pavements there is a ceaseless surge of humanity, so that if you have any distance to cover it is quickest to go by the well-organized Metro. When going by taxi allow plenty of time at lunchtime or in the early evening at the time of the *passeig* (*paseo*) – practically all the taxi drivers are from Galicia, the Basque county or Andalucía and will regail you with a lively critique of the city administra tion during half an hour in a traffic jam. The Barceloneses head their cars into the traffic with insouciance and always succeed in finding a convenient underground car park, or a parking place even if it is three abreast. Do not be tempted to imitate them.

THE OLD CITY AND RAMBLAS

The heart of the old city is the **Barri Gòtic**, the so-called Gothic Quarter – though it is in reality much older, since it is bounded by the remains of the orginal Roman walls of the fourth century. The **Cathedral**, at the centre of the quarter, is built on the site of an earlier Romanesque church and was begun in 1298 and completed in 1450; the façade and spire were reconstructed in the nineteenth century, but on the basis of plans drawn up in 1408. There are three lofty naves; the fourteenth-century alabaster tomb of Santa Eulalia, patroness of Barcelona is behind the high altar; in the chapels behind the altar there are beautiful paintings and tombs of the Gothic period; and the cool and quiet cloister with its great pointed arches encloses a patio with fountains and a garden (often frequented by resident geese).

A narrow alley under the south side of the cathedral, the Carrer del Bisbe, leads to the Plaça de Sant Jaume, flanked on one side by the **Palau de la Generalitat**, the seat of the Catalan government, with the restored **Casa de la Ciutat** (City Hall) facing it. Here, one feels in the very presence of history: it was from a balcony of the palace that in 1931 Françesc Maciá proclaimed Catalonia a republic, that his successor Lluis Com banys rallied his compatriots and that Josep Tarradellas addressed the crowds when the Generalitat was restored in 1977. The Palace, dating from the fifteenth to seventeenth centuries is built around two courtyards, the larger arcaded with pointed arches in the best Catalan-Gothic style. It is open for visits only on Sunday from 10.00 to 13.00.

It is only a short walk, heading west, from the Cathedral to the famous Ramblas. Between them is a network of old houses and streets so narrow that the sun shines down them only at certain times of day and then briefly. One can spend a morning browsing around their antique shops and antiquarian bookshops, and this is also a good place to find an old-fashioned grocer (*tienda de comestibles*) which, apart from selling the whole range of charcuterie — *salchichón, chorizos, jamón serrano* and the rest — together with olive oil, *pasta* of all sorts and canned and bottled delicacies, is also the best place to buy wines and spirits.

Barcelona's most famous street, the **Ramblas**, extends from the great open square of the **Plaça de Catalunya** at the top to the statue of Columbus and the port at the bottom. Richard Ford derived the name from the Arabic *Ramla*, meaning a heap of sand, and it seems that it was originally a river bed, dry in summer (in Spanish an *arroyo*), leading down to the sea. Today, flanked by narrow traffic-choked lanes, there is a wide tree-lined pedestrian precinct in the middle, down which there is a constant procession of shoppers, businessfolk, tourists, beggars, priests and prostitutes. Properly, there is not one Rambla, but five.

Beginning from the Plaça de Espanya, the first is the **Rambla de Canaletes**, so called after its fountain, said to convert anyone who drinks from it into a true Barcelones. Next comes the **Rambla dels Estudis**, once the site of the university, with kiosks selling newspapers and books (many of them pornographic) but now often called the Rambla dels Ocells because it is lined with stalls selling caged birds and tropical fish. Most colourful of all is the **Rambla Sant Josep** (or Rambla de les Flors) glowing with roses, carnations and gladioli, plants in pots, and brightly printed packets of seeds. On the right in the direction of the port and set back from the road is the eighteenth-century **Palau de la Virreina**, so called because it was occupied by the young widow of a viceroy of Peru. It now houses various exhibitions, of which the most important, on the top floor, is the **Collecció Cambó**, a small, but exquisite collection of paintings by masters such as Rafael, Botticelli, Tintoretto, Rubens, Van Dyck, Goya, Zurbarán and others. A few yards down is the cavernous opening of the great covered market of **La Boqueria** (*see* p.188) with a vista of electrically lit stalls piled with fruit, vegetables and fish.

Along the **Rambla de Caputxins** there are bars, restaurants and hotels with canopied terraces spilling over on to the Rambla in the middle, where one may sit and watch the endless parade. Just beyond the Plaça de la Boqueria on the right hand side and marked by a striking design in the pavement by Joan Miró stands the imposing nineteenth-century opera house, the **Gran Teatre del Liceu** (*see* p.48). The **Hotel Oriente** a little further down on the same side is probably Barcelona's oldest – Ford, writing in 1845, mentions it among 'the best inns'. When years ago we first stayed there, its commercial room was still a meeting place for farmers from the country doing business and from the front bedrooms there is a grandstand view of life on the Rambla. Long may it survive! Almost opposite on the other side is the **Plaça Reial**, once the site of a Capuchin monastery and now a broad square with palm trees and a fountain in the middle and bars behind its colonnade (frequented on Sundays by stamp collectors and dealers). The lamp posts are famous as having been designed by Gaudí. Also by Gaudí in the Carrer Nou de la Rambla, opposite the Plaça Reial, is the **Palau Güell**, medieval in spirit with a somewhat severe exterior, but reflecting a creative exuberance in its battlemented, balustraded roof and the shape and arrangement of the chimneys. It now houses the **Museu del Teatre** (Theatre Museum).

The final stretch, the **Rambla de Santa Mónica**, is a favourite for artists to display paintings for sale, for buskers, beggars and formerly for prostitutes (though the area has been cleaned up). With such a cross section of humanity, it is only sensible along the Ramblas, especially at night, to be on one's guard against pickpockets and, on occasion, muggers.

The somewhat florid 52 m (170 ft) statue of Columbus at the bottom of the Ramblas was built for the Great Exhibition of 1888. Columbus occupies a special place in Catalan affections, and although it is generally accepted that he was born in Genoa, his origins are somewhat obscure and there is a strong local tradition that he was in fact a Catalan. It was in Barcelona that he first reported to the Catholic Monarchs on his discovery of the New World. A replica of his flagship, the *Santa María*, lies at anchor nearby in the harbour, and there are splendid views over the port and city from the top of the tower, to which there is an elevator.

Opposite the statue and across the square is the **Reials Drassanes**, the royal shipyard, begun in the fourteenth century and completed in the seventeenth, now the **Maritime Museum**.

t is impressive in size with a lofty roof supported by great stone arches, and appropriately enough, where Roger de Lúria's galleons were once built there are now displays of instruments and charts, tableaux and a full-scale model of the *Real*, Don Juan of Austria's flagship at the Battle of Lepanto. Further to the east and somewhat back from the seafront in El Born near the Parc de la Ciutadella (*see* p.140) stands the magnificent fourteenth-century Gothic church of **Santa Maria del Mar**, at the centre of what was formerly a quarter inhabited by the nobility and rich merchants. Cathedral-like in dimensions, with three naves supported by slender octagonal pillars and splendid medieval glass, the church is lofty, graceful and bathed in light.

The port area, which like the adjacent red light district of the Barri Xinès (Chinese quarter) had become much run-down, has largely been renovated in the cause of the 1992 Olympic Games – the Olympic Village, built at Nova Icaria near the beaches of Barceloneta along the shore to house competitors and judges, has been designed to meet the city's future housing needs. The port has always been known for its seafood, and a new generation of elegant bars and restaurants has sprung up on the recently constructed promenade of the **Moll de la Fusta**.

MONTJUÏC

The hill of Montjuïc rises some 213 m (700 ft) above the port to the west. Its heights command the city, and its hilltop citadel, now a military museum, was built by the Barceloneses when they rebelled against Philip IV in 1640. It was besieged and taken during the War of the Spanish Succession and the Peninsular War, and used as a prison after the Civil War. It was there that Lluis Companys, President of Catalonia, handed over to Franco by the Vichy French, was put against a wall and shot.

There is a cable car to Montjuïc from the ferry terminal at the harbour to the castle at the top, and also a funicular railway from the Metro station of the oddly spelt **Paral.lel** (the Latin quarter of Barcelona with its nightclubs and cabarets) to the large funfair lower down the hill. Otherwise it is a question of a taxi or a long, hot, uphill walk from the Metro station of the **Plaça de Espanya** – otherwise known for its huge disused bullring and the main office of Iberia Airlines.

The views of Barcelona and its port are well worth the effort of ascending Montjuïc, but views apart, it is here that many of Barcelona's best museums, including the **Museu d'Art de Catalunya**, the **Museu Arqueologic** and the **Fundació Joan Miró** (*see Museums and Parks*, pp.138–41) are situated. These and the great exhibition halls lower down near the Plaça de

133

Espanya, used for functions such as the *Alimentaria*, the huge biennial food and wine fair, are a legacy of the 1929 World Fair. Apart from the pavilions now housing museums and exhibitions, a most intriguing survival of the 1929 Fair is the **Poble Espanyol**. This 'Spanish Village' is a life-size replica of typical buildings and styles from all over Spain, each square or street representing a different region. It incorporates restaurants and bars serving regional food and wines and also workshops making such things as tiles, leather goods and wood carvings by traditional methods, and craft shops selling them.

Montjuïc is the main venue for the 1992 Olympics. The stadium originally built for the 1929 Fair has been enlarged to accommodate 70,000 spectators. A new circular road has been constructed to link the other three centres (and to alleviate Barcelona's traffic problems in the future). These are the residential area of Pedralbes to the west (riding, tennis and football), the working class district of Vall d'Hebron to the north (cycling and other sports) and the Olympic Village near the port, an ambitious project masterminded by the best-known of Barcelona architects, Oriol Bohigas and his partners, and designed to house some 15,000 competitors and others, and eventually to add 2000 flats to the city's housing stock.

THE EIXAMPLE

By the mid nineteenth century Barcelona, confined by the strait-jacket of its medieval walls, was bursting at the seams. A Royal Decree of 1859 finally allowed the burgeoning middle classes to embark on an ambitious extension or **Eixample**, as the new area of the city created at the time is known. The work was entrusted to an enlightened engineer, Ildefons Cerdà i Sunyer, who, for the first time in Spain, planned the development as a grid of streets, twenty metres wide and running at right angles. His scheme was criticized at the time – and still is – as being too rigid, but the Eixample is not monotonous and is softened by the plane trees planted along the streets, the variety of architecture and the intersections, which the rounding of the corners makes more like small squares. Cerdà did in fact envisage the Eixample as a garden city, with buildings along only two sides of each block – nor, of course, could he foresee that motorists, desperate for parking space, would wedge their cars across the angles of every one of his *placetas*.

The Eixample lies above the **Plaça de Catalunya** (familiar to residents and visitors alike for Barcelona's best-known department store, the Corte Inglés) and is divided into two parts, La Dreta and La Esquerra, to the right and to the left of the Carrer de Balmes (looking inland). Its regularity is broken by the main avenue of the **Diagonal**, crossing it diagonally as the name implies, and the wide **Passeig de Gràcia**, linking the old city with the outlying community of Gràcia. Most of the Modernist buildings for which Barcelona is famous are in La Dreta. Most famous of all is, of course, Antoni Gaudí's **Sagrada Família** (*see* p.44 for description). The unfinished cathedral, which perhaps mirrors Catalonia's own as yet unfulfilled aspirations, is as much a symbol of Barcelona as is the Eiffel Tower of Paris. Its slender towers are framed at the end of many of the streets, and the leafy Plaça de la Sagrada Família, just north of the Diagonal and facing the façade of the Passion, is always alive with visitors and ringed by coaches.

There are scores of Modernist buildings in the Eixample and devotees of Art Nouveau can spend rewarding hours and days seeking them out; visitors with less time should head for the Passeig de Gràcia. This is perhaps the most gracious street in the Eixample, sixty metres wide instead of the standard twenty, its hexagonal blue paving slabs designed by Gaudí and its elegant street lamps by Pere Falqués, and home of Barcelona's most fashionable shops — boutiques, jewellers, art galleries, men's shops and shops selling custom-made shoes and leather goods. Long ago it was also the home of the Salon Rosa at No. 55, most elegant of restaurants with its stylish rotunda, where the fashionable would go for refreshment after a morning's shopping.

The most intriguing juxtaposition of Modernist architecture is to be seen in the Passeig de Gràcia between the Carrer del Consell de Cent and Carrer d'Aragó, the so-called **Manzana de la Discòrdia** (literally, 'the apple of discord'). The phrase is a pun on the word *manzana*, which means both 'apple' and a 'group of houses' and describes the striking differences in style between three adjacent houses, all labelled Modernistic. The Casa Lleo Morera, adorned with sculptures by Eusebi Arnau, is by Domenech i Montaner; a little further along is Josep Puig i Cadafalch's splendid Casa Amatller, with its crow-stepped gable, tiled façade and echoes of medieval Germany; next to it, the Casa Batlló with its polychrome façades, the curves of its windows and balconies and extraordinary humped roof, is quintessential Gaudí.

Another of Gaudí's most famous creations, the Parc Güell, lies on the northern edge of the Eixample at the foot of the Tibidabo hills. Recently declared of world interest by UNESCO, this was designed for Gaudí's patron Eusebi Güell as a housing development, but was largely unfinished when Gaudí died in 1926. Only two houses were completed, one of them bought by Gaudí himself and now the **Gaudí Museum**. The entrance is

by way of two circular buildings, a porter's lodge and the projected administrative office surmounted by a tall tower with a cross. From here magnificent flights of stairs, guarded by a flamboyant polychrome dragon, lead up to a pavilion on two levels, the lower intended as a market and the upper as a recreational and cultural centre. This is surrounded by a terrace with views over the city and sea, flanked by a lengthy and brilliantly coloured mosaic bench, snakelike and sinuous in shape, and decorated by Josep Jujol.

OPPOSITE
Gaudí's Casa Batlló in Barcelona

FURTHER OUT

Beyond the Parc Güell are the heights of Tibidabo, the highest of Barcelona's hills (532 m, 1750 ft). The name is from the Latin *tibi dabo*, meaning 'I will give you', and derives from the story of the Temptations, when the devil took Jesus to the top of a high mountain and showed him all the kingdoms of the world. Certainly from its terraces and restaurants there is a wonderful panorama of Barcelona and the Mediterranean, as spectacular by night as by day with chains of lights in the velvety dark below. To get there, take the Metro to the end of the line at Avinguda del Tibidabo and then the ancient blue tram up the hill and past the once fashionable *fin-de-siècle* mansions as far as it goes. There is then a funicular to the top, which is crowned by the neo-Gothic church of the Sagrat Cor and below it an amusement park and **Museu d'Autòmats** with interesting exhibits of period toys and amusement machines.

Towards the western end of the Diagonal is the **Ciudad Universitaria**, an extensive complex with buildings housing the different faculties of Spain's second university, and also the 120,000-seat stadium of the Futbol Club Barcelona, one of the venues of the 1992 Olympics. This part of the Diagonal is lined with the great buildings of banks and insurance companies clad in black glass, often set off by fountains of dazzlingly white water. Among them are the city's newest and most luxurious hotel, the Princesa Sofía, and a branch of the all-providing Corte Inglés even larger than the store in the Plaça de Catalunya.

The other side of the Diagonal from the University, in the fashionable residential suburb of **Pedralbes**, is the **Parc del Palau Reial de Pedralbes**. The palace was built by the city for Alfonso XIII between 1919 and 1929. In Italian Renaissance style, it is furnished with beautiful tapestries and antiques and is sited in landscaped classical gardens, which contain a carriage museum. The nearby **Monastery of Pedrables**, founded in 1326 by Queen Elisenda de Montcada, last wife of Jaume II, is one of the finest examples of Catalan Gothic. The octagonal

Entrance to Gaudí's Iglesia de la Colonia Güell

tower is pierced by narrow windows; the church has a single nave and the delicate arcades of the three-storied cloisters enclose a patio with cypresses and palm trees. Off the cloisters, the chapel of Sant Miquel is decorated with murals by the fourteenth-century Catalan painter Ferrer Bassà.

Further to the west and on the industrial outskirts of Barcelona in **Santa Coloma de Cervello**, off the N340 near Molins de Rei, is one of Gaudí's most imaginative buildings, the church of the **Colonia Güell**. Gaudí chose the site in a pinewood, and the interior of the church with its irregular parabolic arches and vaulted brickwork roof echoes the wood outside. It was for this church that Gaudí evolved his system of cords and weights for estimating stresses and designing the shapes of columns and arches (*see* p.42), later used for the Sagrada Família. Half-hidden in the pines, with its rustic stonework, flights of steps, bell tower in Romanesque style and cavernous shaded portico, it resembles a woodland grotto more than a church and is a favourite for weddings.

MUSEUMS AND PARKS

The Barceloneses are inveterate museum-goers; some, but not nearly all, of its forty-odd collections are noted briefly below. The majority are closed on Mondays and the exhibits are often labelled *only* in Catalan.

If the city does not possess green spaces on the scale of

Central Park, Hyde Park or the Retiro in Madrid, it makes up in variety. Some, like the Industrial Park, are not green spaces, but rather plazas with statuary, decorative water and seats for the foot-weary.

Collecció Cambó (see p.131)

Fundació Joan Miró, Montjuïc
Founded in 1971 by Miró and housed in a striking modern building built by his friend the architect Josep Lluis Sert, this is the world's most important collection of his paintings and sculptures, dating from 1945 to 1975. It also holds exhibitions by contemporary artists and is a centre for conferences and talks on modern art generally.

Museu Arqueologic, Montjuïc
The collections range from the Palaeolithic age to the Gothic and contain many Greek and Roman objects from Empúries, as well as others from Roman Barcino.

Museu d'Art Modern, Parc de la Ciutadella
Paintings, drawings and sculpture of the nineteenth and twentieth centuries, mainly by such interesting Catalan artists as Fortuny, Casas, Nonell, Sert, Dalí, Miró and Tàpies.

Museu d'Autòmats (see p.137)

Museu d'Art de Catalunya, Montjuïc
Housed in the Palau Nacional built for the 1929 International Fair, this is perhaps the most important museum in Barcelona with its unrivalled collections of Romanesque and Gothic Art from churches up and down Catalonia. On the first floor there is a self-contained **Museu de Ceramica** with pottery and tiles ranging from primitive artefacts from the Baleares to hispano-moresque and modern.

Museu de la Música, Diagonal no. 373
Installed in a handsome building restored by the Modernist architect Josep Puig i Cadafalch, the museum's collections cover instruments from the sixteenth to twentieth centuries, not only from Europe, but from Asia, Africa and South America.

Museu de Teatre (see p.132)

Museu d'Historia de la Ciutat, Plaça del Rei (close to Cathedral)

The museum is housed in the splendid sixteenth-century Casa Padellas and illustrates the history of Barcelona from Iberian times to the present.

Museu Frederic Marès, Plaça Sant Iu (beside the Cathedral)
Donated to the city by the sculptor Frederic Marès, the museum is located in a part of the Palau Real Major, the former abode of the Counts of Barcelona. It traces the history of sculpture in stone, bronze and terracotta, from Iberian times to modern, and there are also fascinating exhibitions of folk art.

Museu Gaudí, Parc Güell (*see* p.137)

Museu Marítim, Plaça Porta de la Pau (*see* p.132)

Museu Picasso, Carrer de Montcada
Situated in the fourteenth-century palaces of Berenguer de Aguilar and Baró de Castellet, the museum is particularly rich in paintings of Picasso's early period, including the Blue Period and the famous cubist series, *Las Meninas*, inspired by the painting of Velázquez. Also on exhibition are drawings, etchings and ceramics.

Parc de Joan Miró, near the Plaça de Espanya
Popularly known as the Parc de l'Escorxador because it was formerly the site of the municipal slaughterhouse, the centre-piece of this plaza is a pool over which towers Miró's dramatic polychrome sculpture *Doña i Ocell* (Woman and Bird).

Parc de la Ciutadella
This largest of Barcelona's parks occupies the site of a fort built by Philip V in 1716 to garrison the city after it had rebelled against him in the War of the Spanish Succession. The fortress was dismantled in 1868, when work began to transform it into a park. Apart from gardens and a lake, it is now the site of the **Museu d'Art Modern de Catalunya** (*see above*), the **Museu de Geologia**, the **Museu de Zoologia** and the Barcelona Zoo, where a sustained attempt is being made to provide suitable environments to accommodate the animals.

Parc de l'Espanya Industrial, west of Sants railway station
One of the newest of Barcelona's parks, this combines a large lake and lawns and an 'industrial' area with flights of steps and observation platforms dominated by towers reminiscent of those along the perimeter wall of a large prison.

Parc Güell (*see* p.135)

NIGHTLIFE

Few cities in Europe have more to offer in the way of late night entertainment than Barcelona. As far as straight entertainment is concerned there is opera on the grand scale at the **Gran Teatre del Liceu** and concerts by orchestras such as that of the Ciutat de Barcelona at the **Palau de de la Música**. With dinner at around 11 p.m., nightlife proper begins very late, often at 1 a.m. How often does one remember returning from a 'boite' in Madrid with the streets empty apart from the cleaners with their tankers spraying water – but in Barcelona there are joints that do not *open* until 6 a.m.

It is hazardous to recommend night spots because they open, become fashionable and disappear within a year or two. We have listed a few perennials. Many are located along or near a street rather strangely named the **Avinguda Paral.lel** running below Montjuïc from the port to the Plaça de Espanya. In fact, it coincides with a nautical parallel and the name first became popular with the naming of a bar 'El Paralelo' in recognition.

To start with well-known musical halls, there are **La Belle Epoque** with its lavish nude shows, **Arnau** and **El Molino**, a Barcelona institution modelled on the Moulin Rouge, with sails which have, apparently, been revolving since 1909. **Apolo** is another long-running favourite, a dance hall with a large band, where, in its own words one may dance to '*las melodías de siempre*' ('evergreen tunes').

The floodlit fountains of Montjuïc are one of Barcelona's great spectacles at night, and at the **Poble Español**, also floodlit, one may eat, drink, dance and listen to jazz or flamenco until the early hours. **El Patio Andaluz** describes itself as *un rincón de Andalucía en Barcelona* ('a corner of Andalucía in Barcelona'); here one may also dine and watch flamenco – stag parties are especially welcome. Other jazz joints are **L'Eixample Jazz Club** and Otto Zutz's **Hot Club de Barcelona**, both beginning operations at 12.30 a.m. **Otto Zutz** has for some time been, and still is, the 'in' place with the young of Barcelona and only the trendy are admitted. Stag parties, footloose businessmen and others in search of saucier entertainment will not be disappointed. **Cabaret Nelson**, for example, advertises '*bellas señoritas*' and '*espectáculo sexy internacional, y especial porno*' (which hardly needs translation). But the last word must be **Bagdad**, where porn could hardly be harder.

IV · The Wines

The Catalans, never backward in peddling their wares, maintain that they produce the widest range of wines and spirits in Spain. These include ninety-nine per cent of *cava* (sparkling wine made by the *méthode champenoise*), excellent white, red and rosé wines, the madeirized *rancio* (akin to sherry), the old dessert wines of Tarragona, together with vermouth, anisette, brandy and liqueurs.

Catalonia has been making wines since the Greeks, Phoenicians and Carthaginians formed trading settlements along the coast and planted vines. However, it was the arrival of the Romans in force after Hannibal's capture of Sagunto in 219 BC which heralded wine-making on a large scale. Tarraconensis was the first of the Roman provinces of Spain, and agriculture was systematically organized along the Italian model of *villae rusticatae et fructuariae*.

In the Museu del Vi (Wine Museum) of Vilafranca del Penedès, one of the best in Spain, or indeed in Europe, a vivid idea may be gained of the scale of wine shipments from Catalonia to Rome, which grew so prodigiously that in the first century AD laws were enacted to forbid the plantation of new vineyards so as to protect the Italian producers. The wine was transported in earthenware amphoras, of which there are many examples in the museum, designed to stand upright in sand or in serried rows between the grooved planking of custom-built wine ships. A study of Roman wrecks by Josep Brugal y Fortuny published by the Museu del Vi reveals that the smallest ships carried from 300 to 600 amphoras, larger ones up to 6000, and the 'supertankers' of the Roman world, or *myriophoroi*, up to 10,000 amphoras.

Wine making declined with the decline of Empire; the Visigothic invaders of the fifth century AD were uninterested in wine or its cultivation, and the Moors who succeeded them were forbidden it by the Koran — though in southern Spain at least it was a sanction sometimes more honoured in the breach than in the observance.

Revival began in early medieval times, when the great monasteries, such as those of San Cugat de Vallés, Poblet and Santes Creus, began planting vineyards and making wine for the holy sacrament. Indeed, at that time, bodegas generally were known as *sacrarios*, since it was the practice to locate them in the *sacraria*, or sanctified burial area round a church, where they were safe from the attentions of thieves.

When the land reconquered from the Moors in the ninth and tenth centuries was resettled, it was usual for a tenant or *pageso* to be leased land on condition that he shared the produce with the proprietor, and the contract lasted for as long as the life of the vine. In pre-phylloxera times this might well be for as long as fifty years – and, again, in the days before grafting on to separate stocks, it was easy enough to prolong the life of a vineyard simply by planting a cutting and subsequently uprooting the old vine. Relations between the *pagesos de remença* and the landowners who subjected them to a series of injustices known as *mals usos* (including the right of a landlord to bed the daughter of his tenant before she was married) grew progressively worse over the centuries until the *mals usos* were abolished by Ferdinand the Catholic in 1486. Nowadays, with the growth of the *sindicatos* (trade unions) and in the interests of social stability, it is usual for small farmers to own their own land and to sell their grapes to a cooperative or large private firm.

Catalan sea power dominated the Mediterranean during the thirteenth and fourteenth centuries and the activities of the merchant fleet resulted in the introduction of new vines and wine-making techniques. It is thought that the Greek Malvasia vine was first brought by a sailor from the fleet of the all-conquering Admiral Roger de Llúria to his native Sitges, which has been famous ever since for its dessert wine – though production is now sadly limited to a single concern.

In common with almost everything else, agriculture suffered a deep depression during the fifteenth and sixteenth centuries, but viticulture began picking up towards the end of the seventeenth century. It was not a little stimulated by the experiments of the Catalan alchemist Arnold of Vilanova, who, using the technique of distillation introduced to Spain by the Moors, began employing alcohol as an antiseptic in medicine and for preserving wines. By the end of the century large amounts of *esperit de vi* (brandy) were being shipped to northern Europe from the ports of the Costa Brava, while the Macabeo wines from Sitges and a sturdy red from nearby Sant Pere de Ribes were being exported in quantity to Russia and North America as well as London and Amsterdam. By the end of the eighteenth century Tarragona wine was being shipped in bulk, and of the 1,462,306 arrobas of brandy exported from Spain, almost a million were Catalan.

Despite the major upsets of the Napoleonic and Carlist wars

the nineteenth century saw a continued expansion of viticul
ture, and in 1872 Don Josep Raventós of the family firm of
Codorníu, who had studied in the Champagne district, opened
a new chapter in the history of Catalan wines when he made
his first bottles of sparkling wine. By the outbreak of World
War I his son, Don Manuel, was producing some 300,000
bottles a year and was soon to be rivalled by the firm of
Freixenet.

The phylloxera epidemic which laid waste the French
vineyards in the late nineteenth century was not an unmiti-
gated disaster in Catalonia. Before this voracious bug, which
attacks the roots of the vines, had penetrated the Pyrenees, the
canny Catalans made the most of the opportunity to export
huge amounts of wine to France. In 1868–76 average exports
of wine were 1,138,000 hectolitres; in 1882, thanks to
the devastation of the French vineyards, they climbed to
7,670,000. Every available plot of land was pressed into service
to meet the demand; even the hillsides were terraced – some of
these abandoned terraces can still be seen along the motorway
from Barcelona through the Penedès.

Catalonia was first affected in 1878, after which the plague
advanced inexorably southwards at the rate of some 20 km per
year – the worst year in general was 1897. At least the
Catalans were in a position to benefit from the French experience. Some success was achieved by treating the soil with
carbon disulphide, but as in other areas lasting success was
achieved only by grafting the native vines on to immune
American root stocks. The phylloxera epidemic and subsequent
French taxes on imported Spanish wine resulted in the Catalan
wine-growing area being reduced by half, and the industry
suffered almost total disruption during the Spanish Civil War
of 1936–9.

Revival of the wine industry was spearheaded by the producers of sparkling wine, now known as *cava* – a name derived
from the underground *cavas* or cellars in which it is made.
Production is still dominated by the firms of Codorníu and
Freixenet, which, with worldwide sales of some 150 million
bottles between them, have made the Penedès by far the largest
world producer of sparkling wines made by the *méthode
champenoise*.

It is only over the last twenty or thirty years, as a result of
fundamental changes in the technique of vinification and the
careful selection of the most suitable types of grape, that the
still wines from Catalonia have come to be regarded as among
the best in Spain, rivalling those of the Rioja.

In the past, Mediterranean countries such as Spain and Italy

Inauguration ceremony
of the Catalan order of
tastevins, the Cavallers
de Sant Miquel (photo:
Bodegas Torres)

were at a disadvantage vis-à-vis cooler areas such as Bordeaux because of their warmer climate. High temperatures at harvest time resulted in rapid and tumultous fermentation with most of the delicate flavours of the fruit bubbling away with the carbon dioxide. Little could be done about this while fermentation was carried out in the traditional wooden barrels or vats or in the cement tanks of the cooperatives. The introduction of stainless steel fermentation tanks, first employed in Spain at the bodegas of Miguel Torres in Vilafranca del Penedès, opened up new horizons, since the temperature of fermentation could be precisely controlled either by running cold water over the outside of the tank or with an internal cooling coil. This new method of fermentation has been backed up by improved hygiene in the wineries and modern techniques for the stabilization of the wine by centrifugation, membrane filtration and refrigeration. Catalonia, with its cool winters and moderate summer heat, can now compete with the classical wine-making areas of northern Europe on an equal footing, and indeed has somewhat of an edge over more northerly regions in that harvests are ninety per cent consistent (the main risk being from damage to the vines from violent summer hailstorms).

The other great improvement in the quality of the wines has resulted from careful selection and improvement of the vines. With the growing importance of the sparkling wine industry, some ninety per cent of the vineyards are given over to the

OVERLEAF
Vineyards of Masia Bach
with Montserrat
in background

145

white Xarel-lo, Macabeo and Parellada. By 1960 the native red varieties had almost disappeared from the cooler area of the High and Central Penedès most suitable for white grapes, and the old red Cariñena, Ull de Lliebre (the Tempranillo of the Rioja) and Garnacha survived only in the warmer coastal areas of the Low Penedès. The resuscitation of the vines was pioneered by individuals and firms such as Miguel A. Torres, Jean León and Manuel Raventós of Codorníu at the Raimat estate.

The healthiest and most suitable of the old vines were cloned (or vegetatively reproduced), while others like the Sumoll, which produced coarse wines, were no longer approved for wines with Denominación de Origen. At the same time, intensive studies were carried out in adapting 'noble' vines from abroad to the climate and soils of Catalonia. Torres alone planted small amounts of some thirty different varieties from France, Germany and Italy, subjecting them to different soils and micro-climates. As a result of this experimentation, Cabernet Sauvignon and Chardonnay (now used in some of the sparkling wines) are being widely and successfully cultivated up and down Catalonia. Smaller amounts of other exotics, such as the Pinot noir, are also being grown, and it has been found that white varieties, such as the Gewürztraminer and Riesling, flourish in the cool uplands of the High Penedès.

Improvement in the quality of the wines has been dramatic. For example, the *Sunday Times* recently published the results of a blind tasting of fifty 1971 *Grand Crus* from Bordeaux, including first growths such as Château Lafite and Château Latour. A single bottle of Torres Gran Coronas 1971 Black Label was included among them. The verdict of the twenty British, French, German and American experts (including such connoisseurs as Hardy Rodenstock and Michael Broadbent) was that the Gran Coronas outpointed its nearest Bordeaux competitor by twelve points to eight. And this is by no means the first time that a Torres wine has led the field against all comers.

There are eight demarcated regions in Catalonia, administered not, as in the rest of Spain, by INDO (Instituto Nacional de Denominaciones de Origen) but by INCAVI (Institut Català de Vi), an agency of the Generalitat. These regions are Alella and Empordà (Ampurdan-Costa Brava) in the northeast; Costers del Segre in the north-west; and Penedès, Tarragona, Priorat (Priorato), Terra Alta and Conca de Barberá to the south of Barcelona. Plans are afoot for extending the Penedès region by incorporating in it Conca de Barberá and the area of Alt Camp, the proposal being to rename the extended region, which may also embrace Costers del Segre, Penedès Vitícola.

Although some 99.5 per cent of *cava* is produced in Catalonia, it is the subject of a *denominación específica* applying to Spain as a whole.

CAVA (SPARKLING WINE)

When Don Josep Raventós and his successors and rivals first began making sparkling wine by the *méthode champenoise*, the labels, often designed by well-known *fin de siècle* artists such as Casas and Utrillo, variously described it as 'champagne' (French), 'champagna' (Spanish) or 'Xampany' (Catalan). As the Catalan sparkling wines improved in quality and sales increased, the producers in Rheims not unnaturally objected. It was thereafter described officially as *espumoso*, and the term *cava* is of fairly recent origin – the cellars in which the wine is made being known as *cavas* rather than bodegas as with still wines (one of the provisions of the *reglamento* governing its production is that a *cava* must be separated by a public highway from a bodega making still wine).

There are, incidentally, sparkling wines other than *cava*. *Gran-vas*, a not unpleasant sparkler, is made by carrying out the second fermentation in large pressurized tanks, known in France as *cuves closes*, rather than in individual bottles. *Gaseoso*, made by pumping carbon dioxide into still wine, is as cheap and unpleasant as it sounds.

Even the description *méthode champenoise* is shortly to be banned by the EEC for wines other than champagne from the Rheims district. Be that as it may, it is precisely by this method that *cava* wines are made; the only significant difference is in the grape varieties and soils. From the outset Don Josep found that a trio of native white grapes were exceptionally well suited for making good quality sparkling wine. The Macabeo (known in the Rioja as the Viura) contributes freshness and fruit; the Xarel-lo, body and alcoholic strength; and the Parellada, grown in the hill valleys of the Penedès, acidity and delicacy of nose. Various firms, such as Juvé y Camps and Codorníu at Raimat near Lleida are planting Chardonnay and increasingly using it for their wines – Raimat makes a delicious 100% Chardonnay *cava*.

The headquarters of the *cava* industry is Sant Sadurní d'Anoia in the Penedès. It is the home of scores of *cavas* with miles of underground cellars; the larger, like Codorníu and Freixenet, welcome visitors without appointment.

The first step in making the wine is the pressing of the grapes, now usually carried out in a horizontal pneumatic press

PRIORATO

ABOVE AND OPPOSITE
Seals of origin of the
different wine regions

Poster for Codorníu by
J. Tobilla (Codorníu SA)

Poster for Codorníu by
R. Casas (Codorníu SA)

OPPOSITE
Part of Codorníu's
18 km of underground
cellars at Sant Sadurní
d'Anoia (Codorníu SA)

of the Wilmes type or on a larger scale in a continuous band press. The must, without stalks or pips, is then cooled and allowed to rest for solid matter to settle out. Fermentation traditionally took place in oak barrels (now used only for fermenting still Chardonnay wines), but in the interests of preserving freshness and fruitiness it is now carried out at low temperature in stainless steel tanks for a period of some three weeks. Freixenet employs huge 600,000-litre fermenters, while Codorníu deploys batteries of small tanks linked to a central computer controlling the temperature and other functions.

The wine, at this stage still, is further cooled to precipitate tartrate and then filled into stout champagne-type bottles. Cultured yeasts and a little sugar dissolved in wine are added, and the bottles are crown-capped, removed to the cellars, stacked on their sides and left for the yeast to work on the sugar, so producing bubbles of carbon dioxide. The *reglamento* stipulates a minimum of nine months for this operation, but the better *cavas* are left for periods of years.

During its time in the cellar the wine throws a sediment, which must now be removed. It is first concentrated in the neck of the bottle. Traditionally, this was achieved by placing the bottles in an adjustable wooden frame or *pupitre*, so that starting in a slightly inclined position, the bottle ends up on its

Girasols ('sunflowers'), large frames for settling the sediment in sparkling *cava* wines

head. *Pupitres* are still used for premium *cavas*, but have largely been replaced by a Catalan invention, the *girasol* (or 'sunflower'), an octagonal metal frame on a faceted base holding 504 bottles, which can be swung round by a couple of men in a few seconds and achieves the same slow descent of sediment. The last step is to freeze the neck of the bottle and remove the crown cap, whereupon the gas pressure neatly expels a small plug of ice containing the sediment. To make good the loss of liquid a little *licor de expedición* containing sugar dissolved in brandy and old wine is added (the completely dry *brut natur* is topped up only with unsweetened wine) and the bottle is immediately recorked and wired.

In increasing order of sweetness the sugar content of *cava* is:

natur, brut natur	no sugar
extra brut	less than 6g/litre
brut	between 0 and 15g/litre
extra dry	from 12 to 20g/litre
semi-dry	from 33 to 50g/litre
sweet	more than 50g/litre

Although made by the same process, *cavas* of course differ from champagnes in that they are the product of different grape varieties grown in a sunnier and warmer climate. As Hugh Johnson has remarked, these grapes 'produce high acid musts of only slight flavour; ideal base material; the flavour of the champagne yeast comes through distinctly with its richness and softness.' The difference in price between Champagne and *cava* is not a gauge of the difference in quality but reflects the cost of the grapes (currently US$3.35 in the Champagne area and 30 cents in the Penedès) and lower labour costs in Catalonia thanks to more advanced technology. It is of interest that Moët & Chandon, the largest of the Champagne companies, thinks highly enough of the quality of *cava* to be setting up in a large way in the Penedès, while, paradoxically enough, Freixenet in 1985 acquired one of the oldest houses in Rheims, Henri Abelé.

CODORNÍU, SA

The two giants of the *cava* industry are Codorníu and Freixenet, both based in Sant Sadurní d'Anoia. Which of the two is the larger is a question guaranteed to stir up lively and partisan debate in the Penedès. At the last count I reckoned that

Freixenet and its subsidiaries had shipped an annual 5,185,000 cases worldwide, and Codorníu 4,845,000 – but the salient fact is that between them they command some eighty per cent of the world market.

Josep Raventós, who uncorked the first bottle of Spanish sparkling wine in 1872, was descended from a family of wine-makers, whose records date back to 1551 with an inventory of the effects, including agricultural and wine-making equipment, left by Jaume Codorníu to his heir. The Codorníu and Raventós families joined forces in 1659, when Miguel Raventós married the last of the Codorníus, Maria Anna – appropriately, one of the most attractive of the firm's *cavas* is named after her.

Josep's original cellar, still preserved like a shrine at the heart of a now gargantuan establishment, was tiny, and it was his son Manuel Raventós who, with the help of French technicians, began the construction of a new winery and vastly expanded the business. The timing was perfect. There was a sense of euphoria among the Catalan bourgeoisie and middle classes, who changed the face of Barcelona during 1870–1900, and whose prosperity was symbolized by the great international exhibition of 1888, attended by some 400,000 visitors, some of whom were accommodated in a ship luxuriously fitted out as a floating hotel.

Manuel wooed his clientele with striking posters depicting swan-like ladies in flowing dresses and monocled gentlemen in top hats and tails, and in 1898 organized a competition which attracted entries from such famous *fin de siècle* artists as Casas, Tubilla, Junyent and Utrillo. From 1888 his wines began winning gold medals at the great international exhibitions in Barcelona, Antwerp, Bordeaux and Brussels. What set the seal on his success was a royal warrant from the Queen Regent, María Cristina, signifying the Court's decision to replace champagne with Codorníu. In 1904 King Alfonso XIII visited the cellars in Sant Sadurní, and there is a charming photograph of the ceremonial banquet in a room decorated with palms and illuminated by early electric lamps.

Codorníu's establishment in Sant Sadurní can only be described in terms of superlatives. It is the single largest complex in the world making sparkling wine by the *méthode champenoise*. Set in a park with water gardens, fountains, beds of geraniums and other flowers, the buildings were designed by a contemporary of Gaudí, José Maria Puig i Cadafalch, in *fin de siècle* style. The five tiers of cellars extend underground for eighteen kilometres and are served by trains; the old press house has been converted into an arched and spacious wine museum, while the old labelling hall, declared a National Monument, is now a reception centre for the 160,000 visitors welcomed each year at Codorníu (visiting hours: Monday to Thursday, 9.00 to 12.00 and 15.00 to 18.00; Friday, 9.00 to 12.00. Closed August).

During harvest time from mid September to late October, Codorníu processes more than a million kilos of grapes daily. Clearly, such huge amounts cannot all be grown on the firm's own vineyards and most are bought on a regular basis from independent farmers, some of them as far afield as Conca de Barberà. The equipment is state of the art, comprising not only continuous band presses and temperature-controlled fermentation tanks but also computerized retrieval of bottles from the far reaches of the cellars for *dégorgement* and recorking.

Brut wines include the famous 'Non Plus Ultra' (40% Macabeo, 20% Parellada, 15% Xarel-lo, 25% vino de reserva); the fresh and supple 'Anna de Codorníu' (35% Macabeo, 20% Parellada, 15% Chardonnay, 10% Xarel-lo, 20% vino de reserva); 'Extra Codorníu' (27% Macabeo, 23% Parellada, 15% Xarel-lo, 25% vino de reserva); and the deeper and characterful 'Gran Codorníu' (40% Macabeo, 20% Parellada, 15% Xarel-lo, 25% vino de reserva), better suited for drinking with food.

The associated company of Raimat SA with vineyards and cellars near Lleida makes first-rate sparkling wines, including 'Raimat Brut' (made from Macabeo, Xarel-lo and Parellada) and a 100% 'Raimat Chardonnay' made exclusively from fruit grown on the firm's own vineyards.

Codorníu also makes still wines at Raimat (*see* COSTERS DEL SEGRE p.172) and at Masia Bach (*see* PENEDÈS p.163).

FREIXENET, SA

It was in 1915 that Freixenet entered the scene. The ancestors of Don Pedro Ferrer Bosch had been wine-makers for centuries, and when with his wife, Doña Dolores Sala Vivé, also from an old-established wine family, he began making sparkling wine, they named it 'Freixenet' after the estate of La Freixenada owned by the Ferrer family since the thirteenth century (and so-called because of the prevalence of ash trees – *freixes* in Catalan). Like Codorníu, of which it is a lively competitor, Freixenet has grown out of all recognition since those gentlemanly days and claimed world-wide sales of 90 million bottles in 1988 and 83 per cent of the sales of Spanish sparkling wines in the USA.

The headquarters of Freixenet in Sant Sadurní d'Anoia (visiting hours 9.00 to 12.00 and 16.00 to 18.00, Monday to

Oil painting by Waltraud
Torres of the vineyards
at Milmanda (Doña
Waltraud Torres)

Friday; closed August), lying close to the *autopista* from Barcelona to Tarragona and the south, is a massive white building with a couple of turrets rising from its long red-tiled roof, and the offices are housed in an elegant pavilion, dating from the foundation of the firm, with a tiled pediment embodying a frieze of vines in *art nouveau* style. The conservatism of the building belies the advanced technology within. The base wine is fermented at 12–14°C for three weeks in ten colossal tanks of 600,000 litres (an additional *thirty* of similar size are now under construction). The bottling line not only bottles the young wine, but adds the appropriate *dosage* of sugar and yeast, closes the bottles with crown caps, then lifts them by gentle suction, loading them horizontally, a dozen at a time pointing in opposite directions, into pallets, where they remain in the cellars for periods of between 1 and 5 years while the yeasts work on the sugar to produce the fine bubbles.

Of the different marques produced by Freixenet in Sant Sadurní d'Anoia the most popular in Spain is the fresh young 'Carta Nevada' Brut, but the biggest selling in both the USA and UK is the clean and fruity 'Cordon Negro' in its elegant black frosted bottle, aged in bottle for one and a half years. The 'Reserva Real', aged in bottle for about eight years, light and subtle in nose with a hint of oak in the flavour, and the very dry and light 'Brut Nature' (35% Macabeo, 35% Xarel-lo, 35% Parellada) with three years in bottle, are both most superior wines.

In 1984, after the dramatic collapse of the octopus-like RUMASA conglomerate which had cut a swathe through the Spanish wine industry, Freixenet took a step towards becoming the largest maker of sparkling wines in the world by buying four jewels in the crown of the fallen empire: Segura Viudas, Castellblanch and Conde de Caralt, together with René Barbier, a large producer of still wines (*see* PENEDÈS p.163). The premises of Segura Viudas, shared with Conde de Caralt and René Barbier, are off the road from Sant Sadurní to Igualada (visiting hours: Monday to Thursday, 9.00 to 11.30 and 15.00 to 17.00; closed Friday afternoon, Saturday and Sunday and during August). The property is one of the most picturesque in the Penedès, fronted by the green of vineyards, with the blue profile of Montserrat rising steeply behind the old medieval farmhouse which forms the centrepiece of the winery.

There is general agreement that the premium marques of Segura Viudas, Brut Vintage and Reserva Heredad (for all its grotesque metal-encrusted bottle), are among the best that the Penedès has to offer. Jane Macquitty in her *Pocket Guide to Champagne and Sparkling Wines* (Mitchell Beazley, 1986) describes them as 'some of the finest, cheapest and most delicious drinking in Europe at the moment'.

Both Castellblanch and Caralt, the other two concerns in the group, make good sparklers. The Castellblanch 'Brut Zero' has improved enormously since the days when RUMASA exported the wines at cut price to eastern Europe, while Caralt makes a pleasant 'Brut' and a light, elegant and particularly well-balanced 'Brut Reserva'.

Outside Europe, Freixenet with typical Catalan energy is conquering new worlds. 'Sala Vivé', named in honour of Doña Dolores Sala Vivé, co-founder of Freixenet in Spain with her husband Don Pedro Ferrer Bosch, is produced by the *méthode champenoise* in a new winery in Ezequiel Montes in Mexico. Again, in California, a new Freixenet winery is named after another lady, Gloria Ferrer, wife of the present head of the firm. Production is at the moment minuscule by Freixenet standards, amounting to some 60,000 cases annually. My own somewhat sober tasting note on the Gloria Ferrer brut runs: 'Pale straw. Fresh nose. Good, dry biscuity flavour'; Freixenet describe it more adventurously as offering the 'enticing flavours of pear, ginger and toast.' Be that as it may, at the 15th Annual Champagne Tasting (*sic*) of the *Los Angeles Times Magazine* the Gloria Ferrer 1984 'Royal Cuvée' gained the highest award for Californian sparkling wine and the 'highest award for *any* Champagne under $58.00 per bottle'.

OTHER CAVA WINES

There are upwards of sixty *cavas* in and around Sant Sadurní d'Anoia, most of them small artesan establishments which will sell you their wine on the spot – the object of a popular Sunday excursion from Barcelona.

Of larger concerns, the Marqués de Monistrol, an old family firm now controlled by Martini & Rossi, is one of the most substantial (visiting hours: Monday to Friday 09.00 to 13.00 and 14.00 to 18.00. Closed 15 July to 15 August). Situated in the village of Monistrol d'Anoia just outside Sant Sadurní, it possesses extensive vineyards and is among the most atmospheric wineries in the region with a flagged patio overlooked by the tower of the parish church and containing an old wine press. Perhaps the most attractive of its wines is the 'Brut Selección' with its clean, fruity nose and good finish.

'Jean Perico' is made by González y Dubosc, a subsidiary of the great sherry firm González Byass (the Catalan Manuel Bautista Dubosc was the original partner of the firm's founder, Manuel María González). A very popular wine in the UK, it is clean and full-flavoured and excellent value at its very modest price.

Two *cava* firms in the Penedès are held in particular esteem in Spain, where their wines, more expensive than most (but still a give-away by champagne standards), are to be found in leading restaurants. Juvé y Camps, a family firm founded in 1916, owns 130 hectares of vineyards which supply most of the grapes for its wines, made with great care and only from first run juice. Best known is its 'Reserva de la Familia'. Rovellats is another family firm which has been operating for several generations from an old and beautifully restored *masia* at Bleda outside Vilafranca del Penedès and producing an annual 40,000 bottles of *cava* from fruit grown on its 210 hectares of vineyards. It is a supplier of *cava* to the Spanish Royal Family.

There are many other firms making excellent *cava*, among them Mestres, Nadal, Cavas Hill, Mascaró and Mont Marcal.

Outside the Penedès, smaller amounts of *cava* are made in the demarcated regions of Ampurdán-Costa Brava, Costers del Segre and Alella. Apart from making a first-rate sparkler, the Castillo de Perelada, near Figueres and not far from the *autopista* to the French frontier, houses (appropriately enough!) an elegant casino and also a fine library, extensive collections of ceramics and glass, and an interesting wine museum (visiting hours: 10.00 to 12.00 and 16.30 to 18.30; closed Sunday). Its dry, round and flowery 'Gran Claustro' is aged for five to six years in cellars beneath the adjacent and beautiful fourteenth-century church of Carmen de Perelada. The sister establishment of Cavas del Ampurdán makes wines by the *gran vas* (*cuve close*) method in pressurized tanks and its popular 'Perelada' provoked the 'second battle of the Marne', as a result of which the French Champagne companies obtained judgement from the English courts prohibiting the description 'Spanish-Champagne' for all Spanish sparkling wines, whether made by the *méthode champenoise* or not (further afield, the Chileans and others cheerfully label *any* sparkling wine as 'champagne' or 'champagna').

In the tiny *denominación* of Alella just to the north of Barcelona, Parxet SA makes a clean, lively and fragrant 'Cava Extra Brut' (40% Pansa blanca, 30% Macabeo, 30% Parellada). Finally, near Lleida, Raimat (*see* COSTERS DEL SEGRE p.172) has had a great success with the first *cava* to be made with 100 per cent Chardonnay.

Apart from making 90 per cent of all *cava*, the Penedès produces the best of the Catalan still wines. With its limestone soils and temperate climate, the region extends west of Barcelona for some 45 kilometres along the Mediterranean coast and for about the same distance inland towards the mountains of the interior. A century ago it was mainly woodland and wheat fields, but a demand for wine from the former colonies in South America and from France during the phylloxera epidemic resulted in extensive planting during the nineteenth century and there are now some twenty-five thousand hectares under vines.

There are three sub-regions. The warm Bajo Penedès lying back from the coast grows mainly red grapes; the Medio Penedès, at an average height of two hundred metres and with the wine towns of Vilafranca del Penedès and San Sadurní d'Anoia at its centre, produces most of the wine, including the white base wine used for *cava*; the cooler Penedès Superior, rising to some seven hundred metres in the hilly hinterland, is planted mainly with the white Parellada. Its vineyards are among the highest in Europe; the climate is considerably colder and the rainfall somewhat higher, and this has made possible the successful acclimatization of, for example, the Riesling and Gewürztraminer, accustomed to the cooler climate of Germany.

The climate of the Penedès is mild in summer and cold in winter, with frequent snow and frosts in January and February. The main risk to the vines are violent and unseasonable hailstorms, such as that of May 1990 which devastated some 1500 hectares, and to mitigate their effects the larger firms, such as Torres, have installed large rockets around the mountain vineyards. They are fired on the approach of thunderstorms, and the effect is to disperse finely-divided silver iodide among the clouds, so preventing the precipitation of hail and ensuring a more gentle rain. However, with a mean temperature of 15°C and an annual average of 2500 hours of sunshine, the region is exceptionally favoured for viticulture, and vintages are remarkably consistent as the table shows:

VINTAGE CHART FOR THE PENEDÈS

Year	Red	White
1969	Fair	Very good
1970	Very good	Fair
1971	Good	Fair
1972	Bad	Bad

Year	Red	White
1973	Very good	Good
1974	Good	Fair/Good
1975	Good	Very good
1976	Very good	Good/Very good
1977	Good/Very good	Very good
1978	Very good	Good
1979	Fair/Good	Good
1980	Good	Good
1981	Good	Very good
1982	Good	Very good
1983	Very good	Very good
1984	Very good	Good
1985	Excellent	Very good
1986	Fair	Good
1987	Excellent	Good
1988	Very good	Fair/Good
1989		Excellent

MIGUEL TORRES, SA

Various firms and winemakers have brought about the revolution in wine making methods which has since spread up and down Spain, but none more so than the family firm of Miguel Torres in Vilafranca del Penedès.

As long ago as the seventeenth century the Torres family owned vineyards in Vilafranca, and the firm was founded in 1870. In the Spanish tradition, Jaime Torres, the younger son of its founder, was left without a penny, the whole inheritance going to his elder brother. Jaime decided to seek his fortune abroad and worked his way to Havana on a sailing ship. Here, by hard work, he saved the princely sum of 500 pesos, which he sent to an American company marketing a new product, petroleum, asking that it should appoint him its Cuban distributor. The business flourished, but it then occurred to Jaime that the exportation of Penedès wines to the Americas might be even more profitable. Accordingly, he returned to Vilafranca and in partnership with his brother, Miguel, set up what was soon to become the largest bodega in the place.

As Jaime proved, the success of Torres stemmed from looking for markets beyond Spain, and like his grand-uncle Miguel Torres Carbó, who became head of the firm in 1923, he was a tireless traveller. His adage was: 'If you want to sell a bottle, you must take it under your arm' (a precept followed figuratively, if not literally, by his daughter, Marimar, who from her headquarters in San Francisco has built up sales of the

Torres wines in the USA to an impressive 1.8 million bottles annually). Still very much in control until his death in May 1991 at the age of 82, Don Miguel shrewdly despatched his younger son to study oenology at the University of Burgundy in Dijon.

At forty-six, Miguel A. Torres is now acknowledged as one of the world's foremost oenologists and wine-makers. Slightly built, with sensitive features and suddenly smiling grey eyes, he speaks with nervous intensity in half a dozen different languages and possesses boundless energy and liveliness of mind. Apart from wine-making, he has found time to write and edit some half-dozen books. His enthusiasm for wine and his generosity in sharing his knowledge were never more evident than in Chile (Torres has also planted vineyards in California and is considering prospects in China), where, thanks to his example, the country is now producing a whole new generation of fresh and fruity white wines.

Torres was (as in Chile) the first to introduce temperature-controlled fermentation to Spain. The old winery in the heart of Vilafranca (visiting hours 9.00 to 12.00 and 15.00 to 18.00, Monday to Friday; closed August) contained a huge wooden vat of 5000 litres, inside which King Alfonso XIII and his ministers were once entertained to lunch. Miguel decided to transfer vinification to the vineyards, where he equipped a new winery with batteries of stainless steel tanks, more recently replaced by a huge, gravity-fed complex of some 48 stainless steel tanks of 125,000 litres and smaller ones of 60,000 litres, enabling grapes of different varieties and qualities to be vinified separately.

Equally significant has been his long-term programme for improving the quality of the fruit, by clonal selections of the best native vines, by very careful evaluation of the soils most suitable for different varieties, and by acclimatization of noble vine varieties from abroad in the Penedès. These now include Riesling and Gewürztraminer (grown at a height of some 700 metres in the cooler, hillier part of the region), Chardonnay, Sauvignon blanc and Chenin blanc; and among the black grapes, Cabernet Sauvignon, Merlot and Pinot noir. Miguel has commented: 'Fears that the wines would be more or less identical with those of the regions where the grapes originated have not been realized. The quality is the same, but the wines have their own very definite characteristics because of differences in soil and climate.'

Torres offers by far the largest range of table wines of any firm in Spain – all unfailingly well-made. Some, like the 'Gran Coronas Black Label' and newly introduced Chardonnay, are

exceptional. The firm now owns some 800 hectares of vines distributed between seven different vineyards, four in the Medio Penedès, two in the Penedès Superior and one at Milmanda in the hills of the neighbouring *denominación* of Conca de Barberà; and it has recently begun labelling select wines with the names of the vineyard where the grapes are grown, e.g. Fransola, Milmanda, Mas la Plana etc. For the popular, big-selling wines, grapes are also, of course, bought in from independent farmers.

Of the dry white wines, 'Viña Sol', made from the native Parellada grape, is crisp, fruity, and excellent value. 'Gran Viña Sol' contains some Chardonnay as well as Parellada, and the 'Gran Viña Sol' now labelled 'Castell de Fransola', which is aged in American oak for six months, is made with a proportion of Sauvignon blanc. A more recent introduction is the 'Milmanda' 100 per cent Chardonnay, vinified in small French oak casks and kept on the lees for eight months. This superior wine has a complex nose – hazelnuts and a touch of asparagus – round, buttery flavour and long finish. Of the other whites, a great favourite is the semi-dry 'Esmeralda', fruity and luscious, and made with a blend of Gewürztraminer and Muscat d'Alsace; served cold it is an excellent apéritif.

The Torres reds spend less time in oak than Riojas, normally from one to two years. The inexpensive 'Sangre de Toro' (Cariñena + Garnacha) and 'Coronas' (Tempranillo) are full and fruity. 'Gran Sangre de Toro' is even more so and is made from a blend of the native Garnacha and Cariñena. I particularly like the 'Gran Coronas', made with Cabernet Sauvignon and Tempranillo; the 1983 vintage, for example, was round, soft, deeply fruity, and with just the right touch of oak. A new arrival is the 'Las Torres' Merlot, a refreshing summer wine, best drunk cool.

The stars among the red wines are the 'Gran Viña Magdala', made with 100 per cent Pinot noir, and the 'Gran Coronas Black Label', now labelled 'Mas La Plana' and made with Cabernet Sauvignon. At the 1988 Gault-Milau Olympiad in Paris, the famous names from Burgundy swept the board during a morning session, but to the enormous surprise of the French, at the second Pinot noir session the 1985 Magdala was placed ahead of all comers. Gran Coronas Black Label, of course, often outclasses the French *premiers crus* from Bordeaux at blind tastings.

Apart from some excellent brandies, Torres makes a first-rate orange liqueur and an intriguing *vi ranci* (*vino rancio*). The latter, reminiscent of sherry, is made by ageing white wine in the open air in partially stoppered carboys.

OPPOSITE ABOVE
Rocket for dispersing hailstorms in the mountain vineyards of Miguel Torres

OPPOSITE BELOW
Old pumps at the Torres bodegas

Bombonas at the Torres
bodegas for making the
sherry-like *vi ranci*

OTHER PENEDÈS WINES

Wines with the highest reputation but made in minuscule
amount are those of Jean León. A Spanish expatriate from
Santander, he owns restaurants in Los Angeles and after
studying oenology at Davis University in the USA was the first
to experiment with foreign vine varieties in the Penedès. His
vineyards at Pla del Penedès now amount to 158 hectares and
are planted mainly with Chardonnay and Cabernet Sauvignon,
together with a little Cabernet Franc and Merlot, the red
varieties accounting for seventy-five per cent. The Chardonnay,
fermented in wood, is rich and almost creamy and one of
Spain's best white wines. Older vintages of the Cabernet
Sauvignon are huge, fruity and tannic, repaying long keeping in
bottle; more recent wines are lighter in style, though still tannic
when young.

Both of the huge *cava* companies, Codorníu and Freixenet,
own subsidiaries making still wines. Some years ago Codorníu
took over Masia Bach, which dates from the years after the
1914–18 war, when a couple of elderly bachelor brothers from
Barcelona, who had made their fortune by selling uniforms to
the Allies, built a Florentine-style mansion near Sant Sadurní
d'Anoia and began making wines as a hobby. Today the bodega
has a storage capacity of more than three million litres and
possesses some 10,000 oak casks for maturing the wine. Most

famous of its wines is the luscious and oaky dessert 'Extrísimo'; a good dry 'Extrísimo' is now being made; and Bach also produces fruity and full-bodied reds from a blend of Tempranillo and Cabernet Sauvignon.

René Barbier, founded in 1870 by an immigrant French wine-maker, was acquired by Freixenet with the other interests of the failed RUMASA conglomerate in 1978. Production was transferred to the *cavas* of Segura Viudas near Sant Sadurní d'Anoia, where the wines are made with modern equipment and include a fresh and flowery white 'Kraliner' and sound reds made with a blend of Tempranillo and Cabernet Sauvignon and also 100 per cent Cabernet Sauvignon. Housed in the same winery is the Conde de Caralt, which apart from its excellent *cava* also makes good red and white wines.

Another *cava* firm to diversify into still wines is the Marqués de Monistrol. It has long been known for its very dry, light, refreshing and slightly pétillant 'Vin Natur Blanc de Blancs' made from a blend of Xarel-lo, Parellada and Macabeo, and also for its smooth red *reservas*.

Apart from the large concerns, there is a growing number of small family firms in the Penedès using modern techniques to make wines of very good quality, especially white. Antonio Mascaró, better known for brandy and liqueurs and champagne, make a dry, lemony and refreshing 'Viña Franca' and has launched a 1985 'Anima' made with 85 per cent Cabernet Sauvignon and 15 per cent Merlot, grown in its own vineyards and aged for three years in oak, which should mature well. Masia Vallformosa, which also grows a high proportion of its own grapes, has won high praise for its white 'Penedès Gran Blanc' and red 'Vall Fort' and 'Vall Reserva'. Ramon Balada, who owns just 7 hectares of vineyards in the village of Sant Marti Sarroca, has been deservedly successful with a trio of 100% varietal 'Viña Toña' whites made from the free run juice of Xarel-lo, Parellada and Macabeo with interesting contrast of flavours and bouquet.

TARRAGONA

The three sub-regions of Tarragona are Camp de Tarragona, and Falset and Ribera d'Ebre lying back in the mountainous hinterland. Between them they embrace 25,000 hectares of vineyard, making this the largest demarcated area in Catalonia.

Most of the wines are cooperative-made for everyday drinking and lack the quality of those from the Penedès. Among the best are those from Pedro Rovira in Móra la Nova in the uplands of Ribera d'Ebre: a dry white 'Viña Montalt' and the red reserves, a soft Viña Mater and a gamey old 'Gran Vino Tinto Pedro Rovira'.

In the dusty port area of Tarragona itself, the old *bodegas de exportación* once stood shoulder to shoulder. Now installed in more modern premises on the outskirts, they specialize in blending and exporting inexpensive beverage wines both from the area and further afield. They also make up inexpensive 'port-style' wines; the Tarragona or 'red biddy' once sold in English pubs and popular with lemon, was a cheap *clásico* of this sort. Just inland of Tarragona, Reus is a large-scale producer of vermouth.

The most famous of Tarragona's bodegas, the old-established De Muller founded in 1851 and still occupying the original building, is a household name for its 'altar wines'. There is a chapel with stained glass windows on the premises, and the Church requires that the wines are made organically without the use of chemicals. They are exported to the Vatican and all over the world in different styles to suit the priestly tooth — generally sweet but becoming drier. De Muller also makes a range of inexpensive red, white and rosé 'Solimar' wines, a dry and flowery 'Moscatel Seco' and one of the best Prioratos (*see* p.171). However, the most outstanding of its wines are the remarkable old *solera*-made *clásicos*. These resemble fine old Málaga or dessert *oloroso* sherry and include a mahogany-coloured 'Pajarete' and 'Moscatel Muy Viejo, Solera 1926', and also superb *rancio* Priorato, such as the 'Dom Juan Fort Solera 1918' and 'Priorato Dulce Solera 1918'.

TERRA ALTA

To the west of the Ribera d'Ebre lies the mountainous region of Terra Alta, one of the most remote and least spoilt in Catalonia with its winding country roads, shattered castles, shadowed blue mountains on the horizon and townships like El Pinell de Brai, a huddle of old houses topped by a Romanesque church. It is also intensely hot in summer, cold in winter and very dry, so that the vines are pruned low and bushy. As in Priorato (*see* p.171), the wines frequently contain a hefty 15°–16° (per cent by volume) of alcohol, though efforts are being made in the cooperatives to lighten them. The best are those made *en virgen* with only the lightest pressing or without mechanical pressing as *tintos de yema*. As in the Ribera d'Ebre the leading private firm is that of Pedro Rovira, with a winery at Gandesa, which sells a dry 'Blanc de Belart' (with 12.5° of alcohol), a light, lemony, semi-sweet 'Alta Mar' white and a 'Viña d'Irto' *reserva* made from a blend of Garnacha and Cariñena.

The small demarcated region of Priorat (Priorato), high in the mountains, forms an enclave in that of Tarragona. The word means 'priory' and the name is derived from the great Carthusian monastery of Scala Dei, abandoned in 1836 as a result of the anti-clerical reforms of Juan Alvarez Mendizábal and now an overgrown ruin. At least it is remembered in the seal of the Consejo Regulador which is of a ladder into the heavens with ascending angels, marking the spot of the monastery's foundation.

The vineyards are planted up and downhill on steep slopes or old terraces, and the dark slaty soil and scorching summers produce wines containing up to 18° of alcohol. They are, however, of high quality, the most typical being the deep, inky-black reds made from some 80 per cent Garnacha and 20 per cent Cariñena.

The village of Scala Dei, situated at the foot of a great natural amphitheatre of tawny mountains, is the home of two bodegas. The Tarragona firm of De Muller (*see* p.170) has for decades been making a good 'Legítimo Priorato', dark, intense in flavour and of 15°. The Cellers de Scala Dei occupy an old stone building, but possess the most modern equipment and are owned by a consortium of Barcelona families who grow their own grapes. Best of the wines is the cherry red 'Cartoixa Scala Dei', aged in oak and bottle, deep and complex in flavour and of some 13.8°. A third small bodega at Bellmunt del Priorato in the south of the region, Masia Barril, is owned by a Madrid lawyer, Rafael Barril, and between them he, his daughters and his wife look after all the wine-making operations. The Barril wines are dense and traditional, with no concessions in the way of lightening them. Indeed, the 'Especial 1983' contained 18° of alcohol — though this was a freak, caused by the snapping of the stalks during a late hailstorm and the concentration of sugar in the grapes.

Priorato also makes a sherry-like *vi ranci* (*vino rancio*) from Pedro Ximénez grapes (*see* De Muller, p.170).

CONCA DE BARBERÁ

If present plans mature, this small hilly region to the west of the Penedès will soon be incorporated in it. It has a long history of wine-making and in medieval times the great monastery of Poblet, of which the impressive wine cellars survive, was surrounded by vineyards for making altar wine.

Most of its wine is made from white Parellada and Macabeo

grapes and goes to the large *cavas* of Sant Sadurní d'Anoia for making into sparkling wine. A number of years ago, Miguel Torres, in the course of an investigation into the suitability of soils for the acclimatization of foreign vine varieties, found that the land below the monastery and around the old Castle of Milmanda was particularly suited to the Cabernet Sauvignon Pinot noir and Chardonnay; and it is from new vineyards planted here that the grapes are grown for the beautiful Torres 'Milmanda' Chardonnay (*see* p.167).

COSTERS DEL SEGRE

This geographically scattered region, recently demarcated, is important for only one estate and producer, just west of the city of Lleida (Lérida). Wine-making in the area had declined until in 1918 the sparkling wine firm of Codorníu bought the thirteenth-century Castle of Raimat and its 3000-hectare estates. A magnificent bodega was commissioned from a leading Catalan architect, Rubio i Ors, and in subsequent decades Don Manuel Raventós Domenech of Codorníu has developed the estate with advice from Davis and Fresno Universities in the USA by planting fruit trees and some 1000 hectares of Cabernet Sauvignon, Chardonnay and selected native vines. Since the rainfall is very low, the vineyards are irrigated by a system of fixed pipes and perforated tubes, moved forward by what look like huge bicycle wheels. The development has been completed by a splendid new winery in marble, glass and stainless steel, built into the side of a hill.

The Raimat wines are now recognized as among the best from Spain and include an excellent 'Raimat Chardonnay Seleccion'; a red 'Clos Abadia' made from a blend of Cabernet Sauvignon, Merlot, Garnacha and Tempranillo; a fruity 100 per cent 'Tempranillo'; and what is perhaps the star of the wines, a 'Raimat Tempranillo' made with 85 per cent Cabernet Sauvignon and 15 per cent Merlot, aged in oak and in bottle, with strong varietal characteristics and overtones of coffee and tobacco.

ALELLA

This tiny region on the northern outskirts of Barcelona, known for its wines since Greek and Roman times, has for long been threatened by urban development. It has recently been increased in area by some sixty per cent by a surprise decision of the regulating authorities, but boasts only two wineries.

The long-established Cooperativa Alella Vinícola markets its

wines as white, rosé and red 'Marfíl'. They are made from the traditional white Pansa blanca (or Xarel-lo) and Garnacha blanca and the red Ull de Llebre (Tempranillo) and Garnacha. The fruitier of the whites is the semi-dry, aged in oak.

Bodega at Raimat designed by Rubio i Ors in 1922

Parxet SA owns 40 hectares of vineyards and makes it wines, all white, in a modern winery equipped with temperature-controlled stainless steel tanks and refrigeration machinery without ageing them in oak. Fresh, flowery and fruity, they are sold under the name of Marqués de Alella and should be drunk young. The original 'Marqués de Alella' is made from 100 per cent Pansa blanca and is semi-dry. The dry 'Marqués de Alella Seco' contains Macabeo and Chenin blanc in addition to 60 per cent of Pansa blanca and is clean and fruity with herbal overtones and long finish. There is also a round and well-balanced Chardonnay and a first-rate *cava* sold under the name of the parent company, Parxet.

EMPORDÀ (AMPURDÁN-COSTA BRAVA)

In the foothills of the Pyrenees, this is the most northerly of the demarcated regions in Catalonia, but probably, because of the influence of the Greek and Roman settlers in Empúries, the first to make wine. It was Father Ramon Pere de Novas from the monastery of Sant Pere de Rodes who wrote the earliest Catalan treatise on wine-making.

The growers, mostly small mixed farmers, have to cope with excessively hot summers and above all with the winds – the

173

Tramuntana from the north, the Garbi from the south west the Gregal, Llevant, Xaloc and others – which sometimes attain 100 m.p.h. and compel them to stake the vines. Some seventy per cent of the wines are rosés made from the Cariñena and Garnacha tinta, but the region also makes full-bodied reds other specialities are a dessert Garnacha, made by adding alcohol to the must so as to stop fermentation and leave grape sugar in the wine, and *vi novell*, 'new wine' produced by *maceration carbonique* in the manner of Beaujolais Nouveau.

The best-known winery is Cavas del Ampurdán SA, a sister ship of the *cava* house of Castillo de Perelada, which makes the popular white 'Pescador' and red 'Cazador' as well as an oaky red 'Castillo de Perelada' *reserva*, robust and fruity, if not over-elegant. The great bulk of the wine is cooperative-made but there are one or two small private firms making pleasant wines. The rosé from Bodegas Trobat of Garriguella is light, fruity and entirely delicious, and Cellers Santamaria in the village of Capmany make oaky 'Gran Recosind' *reservas*, a pretty dark ruby in colour, full-bodied, soft, fruity and long in finish. It is recommendation enough that both appear regularly on the wine list of the Hotel-Restaurant Ampurdán.

BRANDY AND LIQUEURS

More Spanish brandy is made in Jerez de la Frontera, but there is in fact a much longer history of brandy-making in Catalonia, and it was being exported in bulk to northern Europe in the late seventeenth century. Brandy de Jerez now has its *denominación de origen*, so that it is appropriate that Catalan brandy too is shortly to be demarcated under the name of 'Acqua d'Or'. This is what spirits of wine were called by the Catalan alchemist and physician Arnold (Arnau) de Vilanova (c.1240–1311), one of the most remarkable figures of medieval medicine, who developed the process of distilling wine, introduced to Spain by the Moors, and first used alcohol for sterilizing wounds.

The tradition of distilling wine in batches, rather than continuously in a steam-heated column as is more usual elsewhere in Spain, has been continued by two firms in particular, Miguel Torres and Antonio Mascaró. The premium brandies from Torres – 'Miguel Torres', 'Miguel I', 'Honorable' and 'Fontenac' – and the also excellent Mascaró brandies (of which the cheapest, 'Marivaux', is particularly delicate) are made by the double distillation in copper Charentais-type stills of wines from selected grapes (often the white Parellada). These brandies are aged, not as in Jerez by fractional blending in a *solera*, but in individual casks of Limousin or American oak.

It is usual for the brandy to spend one year in new wood and then to be transferred to an older cask for prolonged maturation. As a result, the Catalan brandies are completely distinct in taste from the comforting Brandy de Jerez; lighter, more delicate and very similar in style to Cognac or Armagnac, from which it is difficult to tell them apart at a blind tasting.

Mascaró for long made Cointreau under licence in Vilafranca del Penedès (Cointreau now has its own establishment there) and now produces a very similar 'Gran Licor de Naranja' by

Charentais-type brandy still at Bodegas Torres

Torres brandy bottles
after designs by Gaudí

steeping dried orange peel from Spain, Algeria, Haiti and Italy in brandy and then distilling it. Torres, too, makes a 'Gran Torres Liquor' in similar fashion and has its own recipe, which includes herbs and orange-flavoured honey as well as orange peel.

Most famous of liqueurs associated with Catalonia is Chartreuse. Not for the first time in their history, the fathers of La Grande Chartreuse found themselves on the brink of disaster when in 1903 the anti-clerical policies of the French government resulted in their expulsion from Grenoble. They found refuge in Tarragona and set up a new distillery, a three-storied stone building with a low clock tower flanking a courtyard planted with palm trees, appropriately enough just down the road from the bodegas of De Muller, the makers of altar wine. Chartreuse was made exclusively in Tarragona until 1940 when the monks returned to Grenoble. For another half-century, the famous liqueurs, yellow and green, were made from the same recipes in France and Spain, the three initiates who shared the secret of the blend spending January to May in Tarragona and the rest of the year at the main distillery in Voiron.

The fragrance of herbs no longer sweetens the air of Tarragona's seaport; all production was transferred to France in March 1991.

V · The Cuisine

In gastronomy, as in other matters, Catalonia is one of the richest and most individual regions of Spain. During the Middle Ages, Aragon-Catalonia under the Counts of Barcelona was, after all, the most powerful state of the Mediterranean, and the cuisine benefited from Catalan maritime expansion and the large-scale importation of spices from the East.

Long before that, foreign invaders and settlers were making their impact on the cuisine. Little is known about the achievements of the Greeks and Carthaginians on the culinary front, but the Carthaginians did introduce the chick-pea or *cigro* (better known by its Castilian name of *garbanzo*), a source of merriment to writers from Plautus to Dumas, but the making of many a good stew.

The arrival in force of the Romans was a turning point. Their innovations in agriculture were not so much in the introduction of new crops but in more fruitful use of the land and improvements in the cultivation of existing staples such as cereals, olive oil and vines. Nevertheless, it is evident from the book *De Coquinaria*, attributed to Apicius, the famous Roman gastronome, that very many of the vegetables, fruits, spices, fish and meat eaten in Spain today were known to and enjoyed by the Romans; and Spain was the main supplier of *garum*, the sauce most widely used in Roman cooking (*see* p.204). Important Roman innovations in the culinary sphere were a shift from animal fats to olive oil and the widespread use of garlic.

The Moorish occupation of Catalonia, beginning with the fall of Barcelona in 717–19 and effectively ending by the end of the century, was short-lived in comparison with the six centuries during which the Moors dominated the south of Spain. Nevertheless, the Catalans benefited from the many new crops and plants introduced into al-Andalus, which included spices such as saffron, nutmeg and black pepper, and also maize, rice, sugar cane, almonds, bitter oranges and lemons. Possibly because of a shortage of fuel in their north African homelands, the Moors' favourite method of cooking was stewing rather than frying, and the *olla*, a Spanish meat and vegetable stew, was the prototype of the many *cocidos, cozidos, ranchos, calderetas* and *escudellas* cooked up and down Spain and Portugal.

The vivid Catalan interest in cooking from the earliest times

OVERLEAF
Shellfish stall at La Boqueria in the Ramblas, Barcelona's largest market

177

is reflected in the *Llibre de Sent Sovi*, a manuscript dating to the early fourteenth century, detailing ingredients, cooking methods and recipes in great detail (for readers who can master Catalan, it has been transcribed into modern Catalan and edited by Rudolf Grew and published by Editorial Barcino, Barcelona, 1979). Of even greater importance was the publication of the *Llibre de Coch* by Maestre Rubert de Nola, first printed in Barcelona in 1477. In the gastronomic sphere Spanish commentators have compared it to *Don Quixote* – and certainly it was to run to a great many more editions during the sixteenth century than Cervantes' masterpiece in the next. Its author was reputedly chef to the conqueror of Naples – Alfons el Magnànim (Alfonso the Magnanimous) of Aragon-Catalonia – for whom he is said to have cooked during the Italian expedition. He remains a shadowy figure, but there is nothing vague about the detailed and sophisticated recipes, running to 243 in later Castilian editions, or the precise instructions for kitchen and household management.

Engraving from the 1529 edition of Rubert de Nola's *Llibre de Coch*, one of the earliest European cookbooks, first published in 1477

Neither of these classic texts – still very much studied by the new wave of Catalan chefs – could, of course, contain reference to the many new ingredients brought back from the Americas by the *Conquistadores*, some of which were to alter the whole course of cookery in Catalonia and Spain generally. Their epic

exploits, insatiable demand for gold and silver, and missionary
zeal resulted in the brutal overthrow of the ancient civilizations
of the Aztecs and the Incas. On the credit side, they brought
back to Spain a wealth of new plants for culinary purposes. The
kitchens of Western Europe remained innocent of such staples
as potatoes, tomatoes, pimientos and chocolate until they had
first been acclimatized and grown in Spain and then elsewhere.

Marimar Torres, author of the excellent *The Spanish Table*
(Ebury Press, London, 1987) has rightly commented that
'traditional Catalan cooking has a definite country flavour'.
This entails the use of local ingredients, particularly what is
fresh and in season. Time permitting, Catalan women, especially
in country districts, shop at an open market with its scores of
stall-holders selling vegetables and fruit, meat and charcuterie,
fish, groceries, spices and the rest. And if the pressed urban
housewife often patronizes the supermarket on the corner,
chefs from the leading restaurants make a point of buying what
is freshest and best at the time of year in the markets.

For anyone interested in food, a visit to La Boqueria, the
largest of Barcelona's six covered markets is a must. Situated
off the Rambla Sant Josep (*see* p.131), it houses some five
hundred individual stall-holders in a building reminiscent, with
its ironwork and high, arched roof, of a Victorian railway
terminus. The colours of strawberries, oranges, red and green
peppers, tomatoes and the pyramids of avocado pears glow
under the lamplight; while the piles of prawns and spiky
langoustines, silvery mounds of sardines and fresh anchovy, or
monkfish, arranged with their mouths agape like a contorted
modern sculpture, positively glisten on their beds of crushed
ice. Aromas and smells charge the air and change from aisle
to aisle and stall to stall – from the earthy dampness of
mushrooms to the fragrance of herbs or from the garden
freshness of lettuce, spinach or broccoli to the smokiness and
spice of cured hams and sausages. And the movement of
people, the ebb and flow of the crowd, is purposeful and
unending. La Boqueria, its stallholders and buyers sum up the
seriousness of the Catalan approach to food.

The basic ingredients of Catalan cookery are typically
Mediterranean. They include olive oil and wine; a great range of
fresh vegetables, fruits and herbs; edible fungi in huge variety;
nuts; rice and pulses; chicken and poultry, especially the ducks
and geese of L'Empordà; abundant fish and shellfish along the
coast; veal, kid, and above all pork and charcuterie; and a
variety of game, especially in the mountain districts, ranging
from rabbits, hare, quail and partridge to deer – and even wild
boar, though this is becoming rarer. As might be expected,

Assorted nuts from Catalonia (ICEX, Madrid)

OPPOSITE
Edible fungi for sale at La Boqueria

The olive tree, from a 17th-century herbal (University of St Andrews Library)

there is a broad division between the cuisine of the coast, based on fish, and the sturdy, rib-warming dishes of the interior and the Pyrenees.

Catalan olive oil is of the best; indeed two areas, Borjas Blancas in the province of Lleida and Siurana in the province of Tarragona, have been demarcated in the manner of wines. In both, the oil must contain 90 per cent of that from the local Arbequina olive to obtain *denominación*. The Catalan oils are sweet and smooth, with little astringency and a clean almond aroma, in distinction to those from Andalucía, which are characteristically fruitier and slightly bitter. José Carlos Capel, the Spanish gastronomic writer, points out that local oil is not always the best for native dishes and that, for example, *pa amb tomàquet* (fresh bread rubbed with tomato) tastes even better when sprinkled with Andalusian oil to offset the sharpness of the tomato.

There are three grades of oil, extra virgin, obtained from the first cold pressing of the olives; refined; and 'pure' – in fact, a blend of virgin and refined oil. Virgin oil should be used in dressing salads and for making *allioli* and other sauces, and for delicate dishes generally. The refined and pure oils are excellent as a cooking medium and for frying; they are healthier than animal fats and may be heated to higher temperatures without burning. The Catalans do not, however, cook only with olive oil and often mix it with lard, so giving the food a distinctive flavour. They are by no means alone in this; the Portuguese make even more extensive use of lard (*banha*), both on its own and in combination with olive oil or butter. Lard has, however, been included in the recipes which follow only when considered essential.

The Catalans make great use of almonds (*amettles*) and nuts in their cooking. Hazelnuts (*avellanes*) are grown on such a large scale for confectionery and other purposes and are so profitable that in the province of Tarragona they are displacing vines in some areas and have recently, like olive oil, been the subject of a *denominación*. They were introduced to Spain by the Greeks of Empúries, and according to a charming Christian legend, the tree, because it once gave shelter to the Virgin, can neither be struck by lightning nor lodge snakes. Like almonds, hazelnuts are an important ingredient of *picada* sauce (*see* p.199). Almonds, first introduced to Spain by the Moors, are also used in the *romesco* sauce (*see* p.200) from Tarragona, and in the Moorish-inspired *panellets* (*see* p.220) made from a type of marzipan and eaten on All Saints' Day. Another nut widely used for culinary purposes, as in the popular *espinacs a la catalana* (spinach with pine kernels and raisins), is the *pinyon* or pine kernel. The cones are gathered from the Royal Pine Nut tree (*Pinis pinea L.*) during the winter and left in small piles until the summer, when they open and release the kernels. Weight for weight they are the most expensive of all nuts (and, indeed, of all agricultural products apart from saffron and truffles). Together with walnuts (*nous del noguer*) and dried fruits, a glorious mix of all these nuts is served as a dessert, *postre de music*.

Apart from gathering nuts in May, the Catalans are among the most ardent gatherers of *bolets* or edible fungi. Although there are hundreds of varieties in Spain, it is only in Catalonia and the Basque country that many are eaten. In spring and autumn the markets are overflowing with colourful fungi which make the cautious Anglo-Saxon, confined to the field mushroom, blanch. Some fetch as much as 8000 ptas per kg, while in a sophisticated restaurant quite half the cost of a meal may be accounted for by some rare and delicate variety. Most common is the *rovellon* (the Castilian *níscalo*); other favourites are *rossinyols* (*Cantharellus cibarius*), *surenys* or *ceps* (*Boletus edulis*), *murgoles* (*Morchella vulgaris*), *moixerons* (*Calocybe gambosa*) and *cama secs*, the fairy ring mushrooms (*Marasmius oreades*). One of the most delicious autumn mushrooms is the yellow-gilled *ou de reig* (*Amanita caesarea*), so named because it was at one time reserved for the Roman emperors. There are, however, a number of quite deadly *amanitas*, and it is on record that the Emperor Claudius was poisoned by his wife, who included one of a poisonous variety in a plate of *ous de reig* served to him. This underlines the fact that hunting for wild mushrooms is not a business for amateurs, even with the guides available in bookshops, and one should always be accompanied by someone thoroughly familiar with them.

Among the basic ingredients used in Catalan cooking are five sauces – though some, like the all-important *sofregit* (p.202), could more accurately be described as *bases* for stews and sauces. *Sofregit* is the *sofrito* of Spain, the Italian *soffrito* and the *refogado* of Portugal, the mixture of chopped onion and garlic lightly fried with tomatoes and other vegetables, of which in 1846 that liveliest of all travellers in Spain, Richard Ford, once wrote:

The almond tree, from a 17th-century herbal (University of St Andrews Library)

It has been said of our heretical countrymen that we have but one form of sauce – melted butter – and a hundred different forms of religion, whereas in orthodox Spain there is but one of each, and, as with religion, so to change this sauce would be little short of heresy. As to colour, it carries that rich burnt umber, raw sienna tint, which Murillo imitated so well ... This brown *negro de hueso* colour is the

Poster advertising *salchichón*

OPPOSITE
Cured meats and sausages at La Boqueria in the Ramblas, Barcelona

livery of tawny Spain, where all is brown from the *Sierra Morena* to duskier man. Of such hue is his cloak, his terra-cotta house, his wife, his ox, his ass, and everything that is his ...

Picada (p.199) is prepared by making a paste in a mortar of ingredients such as garlic, nuts, herbs and fried bread; it is often added to a dish towards the end of cooking and used in conjunction with *sofregit. Romesco* (p.200), one of a number of Catalan specialities first evolved by fishermen at sea, is in its present form a piquant sauce made with a special type of small red pepper and with nuts and other ingredients; it goes well with grilled fish and with vegetables. The Catalans help themselves to *allioli* with everything – as Coleman Andrews shrewdly remarks in his entertaining *Catalan Cuisine* (Headline, 1988): 'For all I know, folks take baths in it.' It is made by beating up crushed garlic with olive oil, but when, as is often done, eggs are added, it becomes in effect a garlic mayonnaise. Finally, there is *samfaina* (p.202), a spicy orange-coloured sauce which has a great deal in common with the *chilindrón* from neighbouring Aragon; it goes particularly well with chicken and lamb, but is also served with *bacalla* (dried cod) and with fried eggs.

In markets like La Boqueria in Barcelona (*see* p.188) you will find stalls festooned with hanging hams and sausages. Some, like *jamón serrano* (akin to the cured Parma and Bayonne hams) and the peppery orange *chorizo* are better made in other parts of Spain; the typical Catalan sausages are *botifarra* and *botifarra negra*, eaten either cooked, for example grilled with white beans, or uncooked as in the *amanida catalana* (Catalan salad), and *salchichón*, which is always eaten uncooked. *Botifarra* is a white pork sausage much like the French *boudin blanc* and is made by country folk or by butchers simply by grinding pork meat, seasoning it with salt and pepper, filling it into casings and boiling. *Botifarra negra* is a blood sausage and differs from the white variety in containing bread soaked in pig's blood.

Salchichón, a form of salami, is the speciality of the mountain town of Vic (*see* p.91). Most famous of the makers is the family firm of Casa Riera Ordeix founded in 1852. The business began with an ancestor of the present owners taking his donkey cart to outlying smallholdings at the time of the *matança*, the annual and ritual killing of the pig in Catalonia, and buying from the peasants any meat which they did not themselves require. The present *fábrica* forms part of the large family house in a main square of Vic. Their *salchichón* is today made from the legs of the pig, and the first step, carried out by a troop of white-gowned women under scrupulously hygienic conditions, is to remove all fat, muscle and other tissues from the meat; it is then minced with small cubes of *tocino* (pork fat, which gives the white variegated appearance), together with salt and pepper. No other preservatives are used, and after the meat has been filled into cases, the sausages are not cooked but hung up to cure for four to five months in a series of airy rooms with widely slatted floors – from the top level one can look dizzily down to the bottom. *Salchichón* is especially popular at Christmas and Riera Ordeix regularly supply Harrods and other august establishments abroad. The splendid advertisement reproduced on p.187 dates from 1906 and somewhat curiously shows a whole waterfall of *salchichones*, conveniently floating towards the al fresco picnic on the river bank.

The Catalans are not usually given to eating cheese (*formatge*) after meals – apart from the *mató* or cottage cheese served with honey as a dessert. If you ask for cheese in most restaurants or Paradors, they will probably produce the ubiquitous Manchego. Good as this is, especially when matured in olive oil, it is a pity that the excellent Catalan cheeses are not more generally available. Among them and worth asking for when in the neighbourhood are: a smoky Vall d'Aran made from cow's milk and a firm Urgellet from the Pyrenees; the creamy-tasting La Selva from Girona province; the fragrant and fully flavoured Santa Maria from Olot; the buttery and slightly piquant Serrat, a ewe's milk cheese from the Pyrenees and Alta Ribagorça; Montsec, a goat cheese made only at the village of Clua in Lleida province, a little like Camembert in appearance, a bit acid and salty with its own intense flavour; and Tupi (also known as Llenguat or Cucat), which is simply Serrat or Vall d'Aran further matured in a wooden container or *tupi*. This makes it piquant and strong in flavour with an aftertaste of Roquefort and of the spirits used in ageing it.

Recipes for a selection of traditional Catalan dishes follow later. Popular starters are *pa amb tomàquet* (country bread sprinkled with olive oil and rubbed with fresh tomato and garlic), *espinacs a la catalana* (boiled spinach with pine kernels and raisins), *calçotada* (made only in the spring by grilling spring onions over charcoal), *escalivada* (fresh vegetables cooked over a wood fire) and *faves a la catalana* (broad beans with black sausage and other ingredients).

Fish dishes abound, among them *sarsuela* (a magnificent fish stew cooked in a sauce of fresh tomatoes), *parrilladas* (mixed grills of fish), *suquet* (fish and potato soup), *rap a la catalana* (angler fish in pine kernel sauce) and *llagosta amb xocolata* (lobster with chocolate sauce). This last dish from the Costa Brava is typical of the Catalan flair for combining unusual

OPPOSITE
Grilling on a *parrilla*

Breast of duck with chestnuts and
cherries at Casa Irene in Arties

flavours and ingredients. Another example is *mar i muntanya* (literally 'sea and mountain'), which is made with various combinations of chicken, white meat and fish or shellfish, e.g. chicken with lobster; rabbit with monkfish, cuttlefish, prawns and snails; or rabbit with pork, sole and mussels. *Bacalla*, the salted and dried cod popular all over Spain and Portugal, is prepared with *samfaina* (p.202); with honey; puréed with potatoes as *brandada* and in other ways. *Paella* is not a Catalan dish, though it hails from Valencia, once part of the Kingdom of Aragon-Catalonia, and is as popular in Catalonia as in the rest of Spain. The Ebro delta, in fact, produces even more rice than the salt marshes of Valencia, and Barcelona has its own version of *paella*, *arros parellada*, made with filleted meat and fish.

Chicken is often served with the spicy *samfaina* and sometimes with a delicate *cava* (sparkling wine) sauce. The free range duck and geese from L'Empordà are usually roasted and often served with pears or chestnuts.

Of meat dishes, the most famous is *escudella i carn d'olla*, a meat and vegetable stew along the lines of the *pot au feu* or *olla podrida* beloved by Don Quixote, and served as three courses: soup, mixed meats and vegetables. There are roasts of kid, especially delicious in the spring, of lamb and of veal. Pork is served in many forms, among them *costellas amb allioli* (cutlets with allioli), *llomillo amb mongetes* (fried escalopes with haricot beans) and *llom de porc amb salsa de magrana* (pork loin with pomegranate sauce).

A dessert which appears on every menu is the delicious *crema catalana*, a baked custard topped with a layer of brittle caramel. *Postre de music*, a mixture of nuts and dried fruits, is now making an extra appearance at the breakfast buffets increasingly popular in the Paradors and better hotels, where one helps oneself to almonds, hazelnuts, walnuts, raisins and dates as a very superior sort of muesli. *Mel i mató* is another very simple but satisfactory dessert made simply by sprinkling cottage cheese with honey. Like other regions of Spain, Catalonia has its Moorish-inspired sweetmeats made from almonds and eggs in the shape of *panellets*, petit fours made from marzipan. A speciality of the new wave cuisine is the sorbets made from fresh fruit or herbs, of which the most famous is the *refresc de menta* devised by that Catalan master chef, Josep Mercader. His successor at the Hotel-Restaurant Ampurdán, Jaume Subirós, has recently introduced an intriguing variant made with an infusion of the flowers from wild thyme.

The *nouvelle cuisine* much influenced chefs in the more sophisticated Spanish restaurants, especially those in Catalonia and the Basque country. Indeed, that superstar of Basque chefs, Juan María Arzak, has gone on record as saying: 'Ten years ago the Catalans, quite without reason, had a heavy cuisine. Now it has changed completely.' It would, however, be a mistake to think that the enlivenment of the Catalan cuisine has been a slavish imitation of the French; rather than this it is dedicated to cooking the best prime ingredients in such a way as to bring out their flavours to the full. The aims of the present renaissance of Spanish cookery have perhaps been best expressed by the renowned Basque chef, Pedro Subijana, as '... the return to simple cookery and the respect for tradition and its rehabilitation. You therefore have on your menu: old dishes, some included more for nostalgic reasons than for their flavour, traditional dishes, but very carefully cooked, and, finally, some new ones.'

The most influential of the 'new' Catalan chefs was Josep Mercader, born in the fishing village of Cadaqués in 1926. While still in his late teens Mercader worked at the railway station restaurant at Portbou, an important communications centre in those halcyon days of trains, under the famous Pere Granollers, fresh from the Hôtel de Paris in Monte Carlo. He always considered Granollers as his first and abiding mentor. At twenty-five, after varied experience in other restaurants, including the Mirabelle in London, he was working at a hotel in Sant Feliu on the Costa Brava, when its Swiss owners backed

Trainee chef preparing salad at the Escola de Restauració i Hostalatge in Barcelona

him in opening what he modestly called a 'motel' on the main road to France outside Figueres. It was here that he began experimenting with traditional Catalan dishes and creating new ones such as the now classic broad bean salad with mint, aubergines stuffed with anchovies, *garum* (p.204) and the famous mint sorbet (p.221) – throughout his life he was fascinated with herbs and their culinary uses. Mercader died young in 1979, but was fortunately succeeded by his talented son-in-law, Jaume Subirós; and the motel, on a quiet loop since the opening of the *autopista* and now more suitably named the Hotel-Restaurant Ampurdán, offers some of the best cooking in Catalonia and in Spain.

In 1985, with the sponsorship of the large wine and food companies, a school for training young chefs, restaurateurs and hoteliers was opened in Barcelona under the name of the Escola de Restauració i Hostalatge. The premises and equipment are brand new, and standards are very high. Its three hundred students must first spend a year studying basics and then specialize during the remaining two years of their course either on cooking, restaurant-keeping or hotel-keeping. The food prepared by students in the kitchens may be sampled in a comfortable restaurant open to the public and is served by their companions on the restaurant course. The President of the School is Sr Josep Julia i Bertran, proprietor of the famous Reno, one of Barcelona's classic restaurants serving impeccable French, Spanish and Catalan food. The instructors are drawn

194

Maite Manjón preparing stuffed peppers

from other leading restaurants, and the students take part in blind tastings of wines, Spanish and foreign, run by the oenologist of Bodegas Torres.

There are reputedly some 10,000 restaurants and bars in Barcelona alone, and rather than rely on our own limited knowledge, we print a select list drawn up with the help of the Restaurateurs' Association (Gremi de Restauració de Barcelona). Outside Barcelona, the choice is our own and is weighted in favour of restaurants serving traditional Catalan food. Apart from restaurants, the seven Paradors (state-owned hotels) listed on p.15 serve a selection of regional dishes and wines, and at some, especially Tortosa, the cooking is good and the wine list well-chosen.

RESTAURANTS

BARCELONA
(grouped according to type of cuisine by the Gremi de Restauració de Barcelona. All the restaurants serve some Catalan dishes)

Haute cuisine, luxury and international

El Dorado Petit, Dolors Monserda 51, tel. 204 51 53
Finisterre, Av. Diagonal 469, tel. 322 01 52
Neichel, Av. Pedralbes 16 bis, tel. 203 84 08
Orotava, Consejo de Ciento 335, tel. 302 31 28

195

Quo Vadis, Carmen 7, tel. 302 40 72
Reno, Tuset 27, tel. 200 91 29
Via Veneto, Ganduxer 10–12, tel. 200 72 44

Classical French and Spanish

Calderón, Rambla Cataluña 26, tel. 301 00 00
Casa Isidro, Las Flores 12, tel. 241 11 39
El Cabaillito Blanco, Mallorca 196, tel. 253 10 33
El Túnel, Ample 33, tel. 315 27 59
Hostal Sant Jordi, Trav. de Dalt 123, tel. 213 24 54

New Catalan

Azulete, Via Augusta 281, tel. 203 59 43
El Túnel de Muntaner, San Marino, 22, tel. 212 60 74
Florián, Bertrand i Serra 20, tel. 212 46 27
Jaume de Provença, Provença 88, tel. 430 00 29
La Odisea, Copons 7, tel. 302 60 34
Satelite, Av. de Sarria 10, tel. 321 34 31
Viña Rosa Rosa, Av. de Sarria 17, tel. 430 00 03

Traditional Catalan

Agut d'Avignon, Trinidad 3, tel. 302 60 34
Los Caracoles, Escudellers 14, tel. 302 31 85
Siete Puertas, Passeig Isabel II 14, tel. 319 30 33

Fish and shellfish

Amaya, Ramblas, 20, tel. 318 27 42
Botafumeiro, Gran de Gracia 81, tel. 218 42 30
El Deporte, Playa San Miguel 12, tel. 315 19 03
El Pescador, Mallorca 314, tel. 207 10 24
La Dorada, Trav. de Gracia 44, tel. 200 63 22
Lemos, Dos de Maig 302, tel. 235 30 26
Mediterraneo, Passeig Colon 4, tel. 315 17 55
Medulio, Av. Princep d'Asturias 6, tel. 217 38 68
Peixerot, Tarragona 177, tel. 424 69 69

ARBÚCIES

Les Pipes, Crtra de Viladrau km 2, tel. (972) 86 10 88. Old water mill with country fare, included for charming ambience and surroundings – and freshest of river trout.

ARGENTONA

El Raco d'en Binu, Puig i Cadafalch 14, tel. (93) 797 01 01. Run by the Forti family, former owners of the Hotel Colón in Barcelona, the restaurant offers Catalan cooking at its most sophisticated.

ARENYS DE MAR

Hispania, Crtra Reial 54, tel. (93) 791 04 77. The Rexach sisters serve some of the best traditional fare in Catalonia, specializing in fish.

ARTIES

Casa Irene (Hotel Valarties), Major 4, tel. (973) 64 09 00. Highly sophisticated cooking in both the French and Catalan manner.

CAMBRILS

C'an Gatell, Passeig Miramar 27, tel. (977) 36 01 06. Like the other two restaurants in Cambrils belonging to the Gatell family, this serves a splendid variety of fish and shellfish.

Casa Gatell, Passeig Miramar 26, tel. (977) 36 00 57. Excellent seafood very much along the lines of the above.

Eugenia, Consolat de Mar 80, (977) 36 01 68. Elegant restaurant with charming service and simple cooking of fish in its natural juices.

FIGUERES

Hotel Ampurdán, Crtra N 11, tel. (972) 50 05 62. Opened by Josep Mercader, originator of the new Catalan cuisine, it continues to offer the very best of Catalan cuisine under the aegis of his son-in-law, Jaume Subirós.

Hotel Durán, Lasauca 5, tel. 50 12 50. Old established family concern, serving good Catalan, Spanish and French food.

LA SEU D'URGELL

El Castell, Crtra de Lleida km 129, tel. (973) 35 07 04. Catalan, French and Spanish cooking. Game in season, mountain cheeses, long wine list.

LLEIDA

Forn de Nastasi, Salmeron 10, tel. (973) 23 45 10. Straightforward cooking based on the excellent local vegetables and top quality fish and meat. The menu includes Catalan specialities.

MARTINET DE CERDAÑA

Boix, Crtra Seu d'Urgell–Puigcerda, tel. (973) 51 50 50. Excellent Catalan cooking, esp. soups and game, in a quiet Pyrenean hotel.

PLATJA D'ARO

Big Rock, Crtra de Mas Nou km 1.5, tel. (972) 81 80 12.

First-rate restaurant with rooms in an old hilltop mansion, run by one of Catalonia's leading chefs, Carles Carmos.

ROSES

Almadraba Park Hotel, Platja de l'Almadraba, tel. (972) 25 65 50. Luxury hotel and sister establishment of the Hotel-Restaurant Ampurdán with the same superlative food.

S'AGARÓ

Hostal de la Gavina, Pl. de la Rosaleda, tel. (972) 32 11 00. The Hostal is the most fashionable (and expensive) hotel on the Costa Brava, and its restaurant offers sophisticated international food, with a few Catalan dishes.

SANT FELIU DE GUIXOLS

Eldorado Petit, Rambla Vidal 23, tel. (972) 32 18 18. It was here that Llúis Cruanyas, a leading exponent of the new Catalan cuisine, made his reputation, subsequently opening other restaurants of the same name in Barcelona and New York.

SITGES

Mare Nostrum, Passeig de la Ribeira 60, tel. (93) 894 33 93. Fish, especially *sopa de pescadores*.

TARRAGONA

Sol Ric, Via Augusta 227, tel. (977) 23 20 32. Best in Tarragona, with pleasant garden and extensive repertoire of Tarragonese and Catalan dishes.

VILAFRANCA DEL PENEDÈS

Casa Juan, Pl. de l'Estacio 8, tel. (93) 890 31 71. Honest to goodness, well-cooked Catalan food and representative list of Penedès wines.

VILANOVA I LA GELTRÚ

Peixerot, Passeig Maritim, 56, tel. (93) 815 06 25. Sea front restaurant serving excellent fish and shellfish.

VI · The Recipes

Note: All recipes serve four people except where otherwise mentioned. Quantities are given in metric, imperial and US measures.

SALSES (SAUCES)

Allioli (Garlic sauce)

Used since Roman times, this classic, all purpose Catalan sauce corresponds to the *aïoli* of Provence and is served with grills, roast meat, fish and vegetables. Purists insist that it be made without eggs, but many alliolis (in common with *aïoli*) do contain eggs — which makes them considerably easier to prepare, but more like mayonnaise.

Makes approximately 150 ml/5 fl oz/⅔ cup

> 6 cloves garlic
> salt
> 30 ml/2 tbsp/2 tbsp parsley, chopped
> 150 ml/5 fl oz/⅔ cup virgin olive oil
> a little lemon juice

Crush the garlic in a mortar with a little salt and the parsley. Drip in the olive oil little by little, stirring all the while with a wooden spoon, add the lemon juice and continue stirring until the sauce thickens like a mayonnaise. This may also be done in a blender or food processor.

A variety of other ingredients are sometimes incorporated in the basic recipe, often an egg yolk.

Picada

This is one of the five basic Catalan sauces. It is made from almonds or the hazelnuts so extensively grown in Catalonia, saffron, fried bread and other ingredients. It has been likened to *roux*, in that it is often stirred into a dish towards the end of cooking to thicken it and enhance the flavour.

For a recipe serving 4–6

> 4 fingers white bread
> virgin olive oil
> 50 g/2 oz/½ cup roasted almonds and/or hazelnuts, skinned
> few strands of saffron
> 2 large cloves garlic, peeled

First fry the fingers of bread in hot olive oil, then pound all the ingredients in a mortar to a smooth paste. Dilute with a spoonful of the liquid from the dish for which it is intended (whether fish, shellfish or game) and stir together well. Picada is usually added during the last stages of cooking.

Romesco

This famous sauce takes its name from a variety of small, dried sweet red pepper (also known as *nyora*). In fact, it was evolved from a dish, *romesco de peix*, made at sea around Tarragona by the fishermen, who invented the sauce to improve the flavour of fish kept for their own use, as not being delicate enough to sell. It is made from a variety of indigenous Catalan ingredients and goes well with fish, vegetables and broiled meat.

Makes approx. 250 ml/8 fl oz/1 cup

> 3 dried romesco peppers or 1 dried chili pepper, seeded, and 1 small fresh red pepper, roasted, cooled, seeded and cut up
> 10 roasted almonds
> 3 cloves garlic, crushed
> 3 medium tomatoes, peeled, seeded and chopped
> 1 slice bread, fried and crumbled
> white pepper
> 5 ml spoon skint/1 tsp skint/1 tsp skint sweet paprika, only if using chili
> 100–125 ml/4 fl oz/½ cup olive oil
> 100–125 ml/4 fl oz/½ cup wine vinegar
> salt

Soak the romesco peppers or chili pepper in tepid water for 30 minutes, then drain and crush them in a mortar with the almonds and fresh pepper if used, or use a blender or food processor. Blend the paste with the garlic, tomatoes, fried breadcrumbs, pepper and paprika if used, and transfer the mixture to a bowl. Gradually add the oil, stirring with a wooden spoon as if making mayonnaise. Again, a blender or food processor may be used. Continue with the addition of the vinegar and a pinch of salt. Cover the bowl and leave for 2 hours in the refrigerator, checking the seasoning before serving.

Salsa maionesa (Mayonnaise)

According to well-established historical tradition mayonnaise originated in Port Mahon in Minorca and, in various forms, is a great favourite in the Balearic Islands and Catalonia.

Makes approx. 300 ml/½ pint/1⅓ cup

2 egg yolks
5 ml spoon/1 tsp/1 tsp dry mustard
5 ml spoon/1 tsp/1 tsp salt
1 clove garlic, crushed
300 ml/½ pint/1⅓ cup approx. virgin olive oil
juice of 1 lemon
salt, to taste

Method with a blender or food processor: Put the yolks, mustard, salt and garlic into the blender and mix at medium speed. With the motor running, trickle in the olive oil until the mayonnaise has thickened, then add the lemon juice and salt and blend at the highest speed for a few seconds.

Method without a blender: Break the egg yolks into a large bowl and beat with the garlic, salt and mustard. Add the oil little by little, beating with a wooden spoon until the mayonnaise thickens. If it shows any signs of curdling, beat in another yolk. Once it has thickened, trickle in the lemon juice and stir well.

This mayonnaise may be stored in the refrigerator in a screw-top jar for up to a week and used as required.

Salsa maionesa verde (Green mayonnaise)

This is a variant which goes well with fish.
Makes approx. 300 ml/½ pint/1⅓ cup

15 ml spoon/1 tbsp/1 tbsp spinach, chopped
15 ml spoon/1 tbsp/1 tbsp watercress, chopped
15 ml spoon/1 tbsp/1 tbsp tarragon, chopped
15 ml spoon/1 tbsp/1 tbsp chervil, chopped
15 ml spoon/1 tbsp/1 tbsp parsley, chopped
salt to taste
300 ml/½ pint/1⅓ cup salsa maionesa (mayonnaise)

Simmer all the vegetables together for 8 minutes, adding a little salt. Drain and rub through a sieve, or alternatively purée in a blender or food processor so as to obtain a smooth paste. Leave until cold, then add to the mayonnaise and stir well with a wooden spoon.

Salsa vinagreta (Vinaigrette sauce)

For dressing salads, avocado pears etc.
Makes 100–125 ml/4 fl oz/½ cup

1 clove garlic
30 ml/2 tbsp/2 tbsp sherry vinegar
90 ml/6 tbsp/6 tbsp virgin olive oil
salt and pepper
chopped parsley

Crush the garlic in a mortar and pestle, add the vinegar, olive oil and seasoning, and beat well with a spoon until well combined.

After pouring the sauce over the salad, it should be garnished with a little chopped parsley.

Samfaina

Samfaina is employed in the same way as *sofregit* (see below) and is made by slowly cooking together tomatoes, aubergines, onions and red peppers in a little olive oil until very soft. It is often used in stewing chicken or lamb, or as an accompaniment to either meat or fish.

Sofregit

Sofregit (known as *sofrito* in Spain and *refogado* in Portugal, where it is also a staple) is a mixture of chopped and lightly sautéed vegetables used to enrich a variety of dishes. It always contains chopped onion and garlic, and can be varied by the addition of tomatoes, peppers and paprika, and fresh herbs. The ingredients are usually sautéed in olive oil. *Sofregit* can be prepared at the start of cooking or the cooked vegetables may be added at the end.

APERITIUS I AMANIDAS (STARTERS & SALADS)

Ametlles fregides (Fried almonds)

175 g/6 oz/1 cup almonds, blanched, skinned and dried
25 ml/1 fl oz/2 tbsp olive oil
salt

Put the almonds in a frying pan with the olive oil and heat slowly, stirring with a wooden spoon until they become golden. Spread on kitchen paper to remove the oil and sprinkle with salt.

Amanida de pebrots farcits (Salad of red peppers)

4 red peppers
30 ml/2 tbsp/2 tbsp olive oil
1 large clove garlic, peeled and finely chopped
450 g/1 lb/1 lb tomatoes, blanched, skinned and chopped
15 ml spoon/1 tbsp/1 tbsp flat parsley, chopped
freshly ground salt and pepper

Put the peppers into a large frying pan with the oil, cover to prevent splashing and cook slowly for about ½ hour depending on size until they are very soft. Place on a plate and when cool enough to handle remove skins, seeds and core, then cut them into strips and reserve.

In the same pan, fry the garlic briefly and without browning it, then add the tomatoes and cook for about 20 minutes until the water has evaporated. Add the strips of pepper and cook gently together for 20 to 30 minutes until all is very soft. Garnish with parsley and season with salt and pepper. A few freshly cut up chives may also be added with the parsley.

Brandada de Bacalla (Creamed salt cod)

Serves 6 as a starter

> 225 g/½ lb/½ lb salted cod, soaked for 24 hours in four
> changes of water
> 450 g/1 lb/1 lb potatoes, well washed but unpeeled
> 50 ml/2 fl oz/3½ tbsp virgin olive oil
> 150 ml/6 fl oz/⅔ cup warm milk
> salt and pepper
> 2 cloves garlic
> 6 slices bread, round shape, cut from a 1-day-old French loaf,
> crusts removed
> olive oil for frying
> a little flat-leaved parsley, chopped

Drain the soaked *bacalla*, cover with cold water in a saucepan and bring slowly to the boil, then removing from the heat immediately. Keep in the water as it cools for about 30 minutes.

Meanwhile boil the potatoes in salted water for 30 minutes.

Now take the *bacalla* from the pan, drain, and remove skin and bones, and flake with the fingers. Put it into a food processor and add a little olive oil. Process briefly. Stop the motor and add a little milk. Continue in this way until all the olive oil and milk has been used to yield a thick cream.

Pass the potatoes while still warm through a Mouli or sieve and mix with the cod purée, beating all the time as if making mashed potatoes so as to obtain a thick creamy consistency. Season with salt and pepper.

Cut the cloves of garlic in half and rub the slices of bread with them on both sides, then fry the bread in hot olive oil until golden. Put the fried bread in a warmed serving dish and spread the *brandada* between the slices. Decorate with parsley and serve hot.

Espinas d'anxoves fregides (Anchovy crisps)

Anchovies are the preserved fillets of the small fry of a herring-like fish known in Spain as *boquerones*. In Catalonia, especially at Cadaqués, the fish, larger and plumper than the canned fillets in oil sold abroad, are preserved whole in salt. Before they are cooked or eaten without cooking, they are soaked in water and the spines are removed. This unexpected and quite delicious starter is made by frying the spines until crisp and crumbly.

Anchovies packed whole in salt are occasionally available in specialized foodstores abroad. First rinse the fish, then open them and remove and reserve the spines. Soak them for ½ hour in milk, then dredge in flour and fry in hot olive oil until crisp and golden brown. Drain and dry on kitchen paper.

Esqueixada (Catalan salt cod salad)

This is made with *bacalla*, the salted and dried *bacalhau*, which is the national dish of Portugal and also extremely popular in Catalonia and Spain generally. It is an appetizing and refreshing salad, especially in hot weather, and part of the mystique of making it is that the *bacalla* must always be shredded with the fingers (hence its name from *esqueixar*, meaning to tear or shred).

> 4 small tomatoes, blanched, seeded and cut into rings
> 1 green or red pepper, washed, seeded and cut into rings
> 6 spring onions, washed, trimmed and dried
> 450 g/1 lb/1 lb *bacalla*, soaked in two or three changes of water for 48 hours, then skinned, boned and shredded
> 60 ml/4 tbsp/4 tbsp extra virgin olive oil
> 2 × 5 ml spoons/2 tsp/2 tsp wine vinegar
> salt and pepper
> 75 g/3 oz/¾ cup black olives, stoned

Put all the ingredients in a salad bowl, add oil and vinegar and leave for a couple of hours, then season to taste and decorate with the olives.

Garum (Savoury fish pâté)

Most famous and costly of the sauces used in Roman cookery, *garum* was largely supplied to Rome by establishments along the Mediterranean coast around Cartagena. It was made in large vessels by layering assorted cut-up fish with herbs, with salt as a preservative. Though hardly the same thing, a modified *garum* is made by the master chef Jaume Subirós at the Hotel-Restaurant Ampurdán in Figueres, to whom we are indebted for this recipe.

> 2 tins (100 g)/4 oz/4 oz of anchovies, soaked in milk for 1 hr and patted dry

2 × 15 ml spoons/2 tbsp/2 tbsp capers, drained
1 large clove of garlic, chopped
25 ml/1 fl oz/2 tbsp brandy
400 g/14 oz/2½ cups stoned black olives
5 ml spoon/1 tsp/1 tsp fresh thyme, ground
5 ml spoon/1 tsp/1 tsp rosemary, ground
5 ml spoon/1 tsp/1 tsp flat-leaved parsley, ground
2 hard-boiled eggs, yolks separated and whites chopped very
    fine
150 ml/5 fl oz/⅔ cup virgin olive oil
freshly ground pepper

Make a smooth paste in a food processor of all the ingredients less the oil, pepper and whites of egg, then reduce the speed and drop in the oil as if making mayonnaise. Season with pepper and transfer to a bowl, cool and decorate with the chopped white of egg. Serve with toast.

Pa amb tomàquet (Bread with tomato)

This is a Catalan favourite, eaten at home for breakfast or before other meals and often served in small restaurants. It consists of country bread, either fresh or toasted, rubbed with fresh tomato and garlic and sprinkled with olive oil and salt. It is sometimes accompanied with cured ham or anchovies.

Xato (Tuna and salt cod salad)

Like various other Catalan dishes, this popular and appetizing Catalan salad was originally a fishermen's dish. Traditionally eaten on Ash Wednesday, it was invented (according to the inhabitants) at Vilanova i la Geltrú along the coast from Sitges, which holds a food festival to celebrate it in January. *Xato* is often served with *truita*, the Catalan version of the thick Spanish omelette or *tortilla*.

    200 g/7 oz/7 oz *bacalla* (dried and salted cod), soaked in
        water for 48 hours, rinsed, skinned, boned and shredded
        with the fingers
    200 g/7 oz/7 oz canned tuna in olive oil, drained and flaked
    1 curly endive heart, washed and dried
    50 g/2 oz/2 oz can anchovies, soaked in milk for 30 minutes,
        rinsed and patted dry
    100 g/4 oz/⅔ cup black olives, stoned
    salt and pepper
    romesco sauce (p.200)

Buy the middle cut of salt cod (*bacalla*), which is always the best, looking for even colour and avoiding anything with yellow discoloration – which indicates that it is drying out.

Line a salad bowl with the endive. Distribute the cod and tuna on the top, decorate with the anchovies and olives and serve with *romesco* sauce. You may like to lighten the *romesco* by adding 1 or 2 tablespoons of extra virgin olive oil and blending well before using it.

SOPES (SOUPS)

Sopa de pilotes a la catalan (Catalan soup with meat balls)

100 g/4 oz/4 oz minced pork
50 g/2 oz/2 oz fresh belly of pork, minced
1 clove garlic, chopped
15 ml spoon/1 tbsp/1 tbsp chopped parsley
pinch of cinnamon
salt and pepper
1 egg
flour
olive oil for frying
1200 ml/2 pints/5⅓ cups chicken stock
50 g/2 oz/½ cup fresh breadcrumbs
15 ml spoon/1 tbsp/1 tbsp chopped chervil
15 ml spoon/1 tbsp/1 tbsp tomato purée

Put into a bowl the minced pork and belly of pork, the garlic, parsley, a little cinnamon, salt and pepper, and the raw egg, and knead with the hands to make balls about the size of a hazelnut. Dredge them in flour, fry in hot olive oil and reserve.

Bring the stock to the boil in a saucepan, then stir in the breadcrumbs and beat to thicken the broth. Now add the meat balls, chervil, a little more parsley and the tomato purée. Check the seasoning and simmer gently for 15 minutes before serving.

Sopa de musclos catalana (Catalan mussel soup)

A variation on *moules marinières*

900 g/2 lb/2 lb mussels
a little olive oil
1 onion, chopped
3 tomatoes, blanched, peeled and cut up
100 g/4 oz/1 cup toasted breadcrumbs
25 ml/1 fl oz/2 tbsp *aguardiente* or brandy
2 cloves garlic, chopped
15 ml/1 tbsp/1 tbsp chopped parsley
pinch of cinnamon
salt and pepper

Wash the mussels in changes of cold water and scrape the shells with a knife to clean them, then bring them to the boil in about 1200 ml (2 pints) of salted water. Remove the mussels with a draining spoon and reserve the water in which they were cooked, straining it through muslin to get rid of grit.

Heat a little olive oil in a saucepan and fry the onion gently for about 10 minutes until it changes colour. Stir in the chopped tomatoes, cook gently until the mixture is smooth, then add the reserved stock, if necessary with enough extra water to provide for four servings. Bring to the boil, add the breadcrumbs and *aguardiente* and simmer for 5 minutes. Beat well with a wooden spoon to make sure that the breadcrumbs are smoothly incorporated. Meanwhile make a paste by grinding the garlic, parsley and cinnamon in a mortar with a little pepper and salt, and add this to the broth with the mussels. Leave to stand for 2 to 3 minutes before serving.

Suquet (Catalan fish and potato soup)

This is one of the best-known and most delicious of scores of Catalan fish soups and stews. Like the *romesco de peix* which gave its name to the famous *romesco* sauce, it was first made by the fishermen at sea by dressing up the less saleable of their catch.

fish fumée
1 litre/35 fl oz/4½ cups water
trimmings from the fish (heads and bones)
450 g/1 lb/1 lb rascasse (if available), cut up
1 leak
1 carrot
1 onion
5 sprigs parsley with stalks
1 bay leaf
2 sprigs mint
juice of ½ lemon
4 potatoes, peeled and cut up

1 kg/2 lb/2 lb fish and shellfish, e.g. prawns and a selection of halibut, sea bass, monkfish or other firm white fish cut into steaks
flour for dusting
salt and pepper
olive oil
300 ml/10 fl oz/1½ cup fish fumée
2 cloves garlic, finely chopped
15 ml spoon/1 tbsp/1 tbsp flat-leaved parsley
25 ml/1 fl oz/2 tbsp brandy

sofregit (p.202)
picada (p.199) with added bread – 4 rounds instead of 4 fingers

To make the fumée, wash the fish trimmings and rascasse. Simmer gently with all ingredients except potatoes, removing the scum, for about 30 to 40 minutes until the liquid is reduced to half. Strain, and boil the potatoes in it for 15 minutes.

Fry the shellfish briefly in a little olive oil, peel and reserve. Dust the white fish in seasoned flour. This is done most easily by putting the fish and the flour into a large plastic bag and shaking gently. Take out the fish and fry, a few pieces at a time, in hot olive oil until golden. Put on to a plate and when cool enough remove bones and skin and break into smaller pieces with the fingers. Return shellfish and fish to the frying pan, add garlic, parsley and brandy and flambé. Now add the *sofregit* and the *picada* with the extra fried bread, and transfer to the pan with the *fumée* and potatoes. Check the seasoning, stir well and heat together until very hot for 5 to 8 minutes for the flavours to mingle.

HORTALISSA (VEGETABLES)

Bolets amb pernil (Wild mushrooms with ham)

Bolets is the Catalan name for edible fungi in general. There is a range of hundreds (*see* p.185) and the gathering of rare varieties is a national pastime. The best type of ham for this recipe is the cured *jamón serrano* (*see* p.188); failing this use Parma or Bayonne ham.

In Catalonia most mushroom dishes are cooked *a la parrilla* (on a grid over a charcoal fire).

150 g/5 oz/5 oz *jamón serrano*, cut up
15 ml spoon/1 tbsp/1 tbsp olive oil
450 g/1 lb/1 lb *bolets* (wild mushrooms), uncut unless large
15 ml spoon/1 tbsp/1 tbsp breadcrumbs
2 cloves garlic, finely chopped
2 × 15 ml spoons/2 tbsp/2 tbsp flat-leaved parsley, chopped
black pepper, freshly ground

Fry the *jamón serrano* in the oil for 5 minutes, then add the *bolets* and stir with a wooden spoon. After a further 4 to 5 minutes add the breadcrumbs, garlic and half of the parsley. Cook for about 15 minutes, depending on the size of the mushrooms, until very tender. Season with freshly ground pepper (but *not* with salt, because the ham is salty enough) and garnish with the parsley.

This is a dish prepared only in the spring and is made very simply by splitting spring onions, brushing them with olive oil and charcoal grilling them. They are eaten with the fingers, dipped into *allioli* (p.199) or *salsa romesco* (p.200).

Put like this, *calçotada* sounds nothing very much out of the ordinary – but this is to reckon without the fact that a *calçotada* is a communal activity, a celebration with the more partici-pants the better, and that the *calçots* bear little relation to ordinary onions. After harvesting in early summer they are stored and allowed to sprout, and are replanted in late August or early September. Earth is packed around the new shoots, and when finally harvested in the following early spring they are milder and sweeter than ordinary onions and quite half the stems are bleached.

The headquarters of the cult is the town of Valls, near Tarragona, where the restaurants are packed during the season from January until the end of April, and the *calçots* are grilled an hour or more before serving and left tightly wrapped, so making them even more tender.

Escalivada

A favourite Catalan starter, especially in summer, delicious when made with really fresh vegetables. *Escalivada* should properly be cooked in hot ashes or on a *parrilla* over a wood fire, when the vegetables take on an inimitable smoky flavour.

    2 large tomatoes, cut in half
    2 green peppers, cored, seeded and cut in half lengthwise
    2 red peppers, cored, seeded and cut in half lengthwise
    2 aubergines, cut lengthwise
    2 small onions
    2 × 15 ml spoons/2 tbsp/2 tbsp olive oil for brushing
        vegetables
    2 × 15 ml spoons/2 tbsp/2 tbsp virgin olive oil
    salt and pepper

Paint the vegetables with olive oil, place them on a baking tray in a hot oven (180°C, 350°F, Gas 4) and bake for between 45 minutes and 1 hour depending on size until they are soft and the skin browns. Remove the tomatoes after the first ½ hour. When sufficiently cool, skin the vegetables with the fingers, then cut them into thin strips, put in a serving dish and sprinkle with virgin olive oil, salt and freshly ground pepper. Decorate with a few anchovies and serve with fresh bread.

Espinacs a la catalana (Spinach Catalan style)

This is a dish often served as a starter in country restaurants and making use of the pine kernels so often used in Catalan cookery.

2 × 15 ml spoons/2 tbsp/2 tbsp olive oil
2 cloves garlic, finely chopped
2 anchovies, soaked in milk for ½ hour and cut up
1 kg/2 lb/2 lb spinach or Swiss chard, boiled in salted water
  and well-drained
50 g/2 oz/⅓ cup pine kernels
50 g/2 oz/¼ cup raisins
salt and freshly ground pepper

Heat the oil in a pan and fry the garlic briefly taking care not to blacken it. Add the anchovies and spinach, stir gently while adding the pine kernels and raisins. Season with salt and pepper and cook on a low heat for about 10 minutes until very tender.

Favas a la catalana (Broad beans Catalan style)

The beans are cooked with chopped bacon and often served with the delicate *botifarra* sausage.

4 × 15 ml spoons/4 tbsp/4 tbsp olive oil
200 g/7 oz/7 oz belly of pork, thickly sliced
2 cloves garlic, chopped
small bunch spring onions or very small leeks, whites only,
  washed and cut up
1 kg/2 lb/2 lb fresh broad beans, shelled
2 × 15 ml/2 tbsp/2 tbsp fresh mint, chopped
1 bay leaf
5 ml spoon/1 tsp/1 tsp *anis*
150 ml/5 fl oz/⅔ cup *vi ranci* (*see* p.167)
200 ml/7 fl oz/1 cup stock or water
salt and freshly ground pepper
pinch of sugar

Heat the olive oil in a saucepan, then add the belly of pork and garlic and fry until the meat is brown. Put in the spring onions and fry gently for a little longer. Now add the broad beans, mint, bay leaf, wine, stock or water, and *botifarra*. Stir well and season with salt and pepper and a pinch of sugar, then bring to the boil, cover the pan tightly with foil and close with the lid. Occasionally shaking the pan, simmer for 15 to 20 minutes until the contents are very tender and the stock has completely evaporated. Take out the *botifarra* and slice it, and serve the beans with the slices of sausage and belly of pork on top.

Parrillada de peix amb salsa romesco (Mixed grilled fish with Romesco sauce)

This dish is at its best in Catalonia when the fish are grilled over a wood fire. In making it, you must obviously choose from the fish available at the time.

    4 scampi
    4 large prawns
    8 mussels, well scraped and washed
    8 clams, well scraped and washed
    4 medium slices sea bass
    4 red mullet
    4 slices of hake
    olive oil
    salt

The fish are simply sprinkled with a little olive oil and grilled, preferably on a *parrilla*, a grid placed over a bed of glowing charcoal – use a barbecue if you have one.

Salsa romesco (p.200) is served on the side.

Rap a la catalana (Angler fish in pine kernel sauce)

The tail of the large and ugly angler fish makes good eating and its flavour has been compared with that of lobster, especially when cooked and served cold with chopped raw onions, parsley and shellfish. The recipe which follows is another gastronomic delight.

    4 angler fish steaks 2.5 cm (1 in) thick
    salt and pepper
    45 ml/3 tbsp/3 tbsp olive oil
    1 slice bread 1.25 cm/½ in. thick
    1 clove garlic, chopped
    1 sprig parsley, chopped
    50 g/2 oz/⅓ cup pine kernels
    few strands of saffron
    1 onion, chopped
    450 g/1 lb/1 lb tomatoes, blanched, skinned and chopped

Put the fish in an ovenproof dish, sprinkle with salt and pepper and leave until needed.

Meanwhile, heat the oil in a pan and fry the bread, garlic, parsley and pine kernels for a few minutes until golden brown. Remove with a slotted spoon and reserve the oil. Transfer the mixture to a mortar, add the saffron and grind to a paste, then dissolve in a little hot water. In the oil remaining in the pan, fry the onion and tomatoes for 10–15 minutes, and make a purée either by rubbing the vegetables through a sieve or putting in a blender or food processor. Mix this with the *picada* from the mortar, season with salt and pepper, and daub on top of the fish. Cook in a fairly hot oven (190°C, 375°F, Gas 5) for 20 minutes until the fish is well cooked. Serve from the ovenproof dish.

Sarsuela de marisc a l̀a catalana (Shellfish stew Catalan style)

Sarsuela (perhaps more familiar in the Castilian spelling 'zarzuela') means a variety show, and you may ring the changes on this magnificent fish stew, provided that any white fish used is firm and does not disintegrate in cooking.

Serves 6

12 clams or 24 mussels, well scrubbed and washed in cold water
100 ml/4 fl oz/½ cup olive oil
1 onion, chopped
250 g/9 oz/9 oz squid, cleaned and cut into rings
250 g/9 oz/9 oz sea bass or hake, sliced
250 g/9 oz/9 oz angler fish, sliced
250 g/9 oz/9 oz prawns in shell, boiled
8 scampi in shell, boiled
30 ml/2 tbsp/2 tbsp Spanish brandy
1 clove garlic, crushed
15 ml/1 tbsp/1 tbsp tomato purée
50 ml/2 fl oz/¼ cup dry white wine
salt and pepper
15 ml spoon/1 tbsp/1 tbsp chopped parsley
4 fingers fried white bread, without crusts
few strands saffron
12 roasted almonds, skinned

Bring the clams to boil in water, leave them until they open, then drain and reserve them with the stock.

Heat the olive oil in a large, deep casserole, fry the onion for 10 minutes, then add the squid, sea bass or hake, angler fish, the prawns and scampi, and fry together until brown. Pour in the brandy and flambé. Add the garlic, tomato purée, wine and reserved stock. Season with salt, pepper and parsley, stir together well and cook slowly for 20 minutes, uncovered, adding a little hot water if necessary. Ten minutes before removing from the heat, add the clams. Grind the fresh bread, saffron and almonds to a paste, dissolve with a little of the stock, and stir this *picada* into the stew. Serve immediately.

Oca amb peres (Goose with pears)

Goose is a favourite Christmas dish in Catalonia and is served with pears. In the Ampurdán region near the Pyrenees, the geese range at will. Small, with dark gamey meat, they are eaten all year round.
Serves 6

1 goose of about 3½–4½ kg (7½–10 lbs) after trussing
1 lemon, cut in half

Stuffing
1 onion, finely chopped
200 g/7 oz/7 oz bacon, chopped
2 sticks celery, finely chopped
30 ml/2 tbsp/2 tbsp olive oil
the goose liver, chopped
225 g/8 oz/2¼ cups fresh breadcrumbs
2 cloves garlic, finely chopped
2 eggs, beaten
2 cooking apples, diced
100 g/4 oz/⅔ cup ground pine kernels
15 ml spoon/1 tbsp/1 tbsp chopped parsley
salt and freshly ground pepper
juice of ½ lemon

Gravy
giblets of goose
bouquet garni
600 ml/1 pint/2⅔ cups water
2 × 5 ml spoons/2 tsp/2 tsp cornflour
25 ml/1 fl oz/2 tbsp oloroso sherry
salt and pepper

Garnish
6 pears, peeled and cored, stalks left on the pears
300 ml/½ pint/1⅓ cup dry white wine
50 ml/2 fl oz/¼ cup sweet oloroso sherry
275 g/10 oz/1¼ cup caster sugar
1 cinnamon stick

Rub the outside of the goose with the lemon, then prick it and place on a rack in a shallow roasting tin. Put in a fairly hot oven (200°C, 400°F, Gas 6) and cook for 15 minutes, when the fat will begin to run out. Discard the fat or reserve as required – I use it for roasting potatoes. Repeat the operation; the goose is now ready for stuffing.

To make the stuffing, fry the onion, bacon and celery in hot olive oil until transparent. Add the goose liver and fry a little longer, leaving the inside of the liver pink. Mix well with the remaining ingredients, and use to stuff the goose from the neck downwards, securing it with a thin skewer. Return to a fairly hot oven (200°C, 400°F, Gas 6) for 15 minutes, then reduce the heat to warm (160°C, 325°F, Gas 3) and cook for 25 minutes a pound – slow roasting makes the goose juicier.

To make the gravy, cook the giblets over heat with the *bouquet garni* and water, until the liquid is reduced to 300 ml/ ½ pint/1⅓ cup, and reserve. Skim what fat remains in the roasting tin, add a little cornflour, stirring well, and moisten with the reserved giblet stock and the oloroso sherry. Cook for 1–2 minutes until well blended and heated through, and season with salt and pepper to taste.

Make the garnish by gently simmering the pears for about 40 minutes with the wine, sherry, sugar and cinnamon stick until transparent. Drain, reduce the syrup, pour it over the pears and arrange them around the bird on a serving dish.

Serve with roast potatoes and peas.

Anec amb figues (Duck with figs)

We are indebted for this recipe to Marimar Torres, from whose book, *The Spanish Table* (London, 1987), it is reproduced:

This is a delightful example of the traditional Catalan way to cook meats or poultry with fruits. Some of the finest ducks I've eaten come from L'Empordà, the bountiful region in northeast Catalonia, and are often cooked with pears, apples or other fruits.

Agut d'Avignon, the outstanding restaurant in the picturesque old part of Barcelona, near the Ramblas promenade, features duck with figs among other classic specialities of L'Empordà. The late owner Ramon Cabau told me he prefers to make the dish with dried figs, although I've made it with both fresh and dried and enjoyed them equally – but following his advice, my recipe calls for dried figs.

Serves 4

225 g/8 oz/1¼ cup dried figs
1.8–2.3 kg/4–5 lb duck, cut into 4 serving pieces, liver, fat, wings, back and neck reserved (if necessary substitute 3 chicken livers for the duck liver)

For the essence
reserved wings, back and neck of the duck
600 ml/1 pint/2⅔ cup brown veal stock

For the duck
salt and freshly ground black pepper
225 ml/8 fl oz/1 cup dry Spanish sherry, preferably amontillado or a dry oloroso

For the sauce
zest and juice of 1 large orange
30 ml/2 tbsp/2 tbsp finest-quality Spanish brandy
pinch ground cinnamon

Cover the figs with 225 ml/8 fl oz/1 cup boiling water and soak for 2 hours. Stem the figs and reserve the figs and water.

To prepare the essence: Remove the fat from the duck, and most of the skin from reserved wings, back and neck; cut these into small pieces. Fry in a frying pan with 15–30 ml (1–2 tbsp) duck fat, stirring around until they are very brown. Transfer the duck pieces to a medium saucepan. Pour off the fat from the frying pan and deglaze with about 125 ml/4 fl oz/½ cup of the stock. Pour the mixture into the saucepan. Add some more stock and simmer, uncovered, over a very low heat. Keep turning the pieces over and adding more stock, little by little, as it evaporates. Cook for about 2 hours, or until reduced to 225 ml/8 fl oz/1 cup. Strain the essence and reserve. Discard the bones.

To cook the duck: Pat the duck pieces dry with kitchen paper and season with salt and pepper. In a frying pan with a lid, heat some of the duck fat and, over a medium to high heat, brown the duck quarters. Pour off the fat, add 125 ml/4 fl oz/½ cup of the sherry, cover tightly with a double thickness of foil and the lid. Braise for 45 minutes over a low heat.

To prepare the sauce: Simmer the liver in 50–125 ml/2–4 fl oz/¼–½ cup reserved fig-water – just to cover – for 15 minutes. In a food processor or blender, purée the drained liver with 4 of the figs; add the orange zest and juice, brandy, cinnamon and liquid from simmering the livers. Reserve the sauce.

To assemble the dish: Set the duck quarters aside and skim the contents of the pan. Add the remaining sherry and cook until reduced by about half. Stir in the reserved sauce, duck essence and fig-water. Return the duck to the pan. Add the remaining figs, cover and cook for 20 minutes. Remove the duck and figs to a serving platter and keep warm.

Reduce the sauce further, if necessary, to desired consistency. Taste for seasoning. Pour some sauce over the duck and hand the remaining sauce separately in a sauce boat.

Perdiu a la catalana (Partridge Catalan style)

As in Spain generally, *la caça* is a national institution in Catalonia, and rough shooting is jealously preserved. The Sunday silence of the countryside is punctuated by the crack of guns, and towards evening the little groups of hunters return with their pouches full of rabbit (*connil*), hare (*llebre*), quail (*guattla*), pigeon (*colomi*), wild duck (*anec salvatge*) and partridge (*perdiu*).

per person
  1 partridge
  15 ml/1 tbsp/1 tbsp olive oil
  2 × 5 ml spoons/2 tsp/2 tsp flour
  450 ml/15 fl oz/2 cups meat or game stock
  salt and pepper
  bouquet garni of bay leaf, thyme and origanum
  2 cloves garlic, chopped
  2 slices lemon

Brown the partridge in hot olive oil and put it into a saucepan. Using the same oil and pan, stir in the flour and when it has soaked up the oil, add the meat stock, a little pepper and salt, the *bouquet garni* and garlic. Stir together, then pour the liquid over the partridge and cook very slowly for about an hour or until the bird is tender. Serve on a dish decorated with slices of lemon.

Pollastre amb Samfaina (Chicken in Chanfaina sauce)

A method of cooking chicken in a piquant sauce somewhat reminiscent of the *chilindrón* from neighbouring Aragon.

  olive oil
  3 aubergines, cut up
  2 red or green peppers, blanched, seeded and cut up
  2 onions, chopped
  450 g/1 lb/1 lb tomatoes, blanched, skinned and cut up
  2 cloves garlic, chopped
  150 ml/5 fl oz/2⁄3 cup dry white wine
  1 bay leaf
  thyme
  salt
  black pepper
  1½ kg/3 lb/3 lb chicken, cut up
  flour for dredging
  squares of fried bread

Heat half of the oil in a pan and fry together the cut-up aubergines, peppers and onions for some 10 minutes. Drain off the excess oil, add the chopped tomatoes and garlic and cook gently for another 10 minutes until the tomatoes are soft. Now stir in the wine, herbs and spices, remove from the heat and transfer to a stewpot.

Heat the remaining half of the oil in the same frying pan, dredge the pieces of chicken in flour, brown them and then transfer them with a slotted spoon to the stewpot. Cook slowly above the heat for 1 hour or until the chicken is tender, then serve surrounded by squares of fried bread.

Pollastre amb gambes (Chicken with prawns)

4 × 15 ml spoons/4 tbsp/4 tbsp olive oil
flour for dusting
2 chicken breasts, cut into 4 pieces and dredged in flour
1 small onion, finely chopped
2 cloves garlic, finely chopped
150 ml/5 fl oz/⅔ cup Catalan brandy
15 ml spoon/1 tbsp/1 tbsp cornflour
300 ml/10 fl oz/1⅓ cup chicken stock
salt and pepper
30 ml/2 tbsp/2 tbsp flat parsley, finely chopped
450 g/1 lb/1 lb fresh prawns, boiled and peeled

Heat the olive oil in a large casserole, brown the breasts of chicken, remove and reserve. In the same pan fry the onion until soft, then add the garlic, stirring well, and cook for one minute. Pour in the brandy and flame, stirring until the flames subside. Stir in the cornflour, add the chicken stock and season to taste with freshly ground salt and pepper. Now add half of the parsley and the chicken pieces and cook very slowly for about 20 minutes until the chicken is very tender, adding the prawns 5 minutes before the chicken is ready, and stirring gently together. Garnish with the remaining parsley and serve.

CARN (MEAT)

Costellas amb allioli (Barbecued ribs of pork with *allioli* sauce)

This recipe is for a *parrillada* or charcoal grill and works well with a barbecue.

16 ribs of pork on the bone
a little olive oil
salt
salsa allioli (p.199)

Separate the ribs with a knife, place them between greaseproof paper and flatten them with the side of a meat cleaver. The butcher can do this for you. Brush with oil, sprinkle with a little salt, and grill until very brown. Serve with *allioli* sauce on the side.

PLATS MIXTS (MIXED DISHES)

Escudella i carn d'olla (Meat and vegetable stew)

Very similar stews of meat, vegetable and pulses, served as several courses, are found in France (*pot-au-feu*); in Italy (*bolliti*) and in Spain and Portugal (*cocidos* and *cozidos*). This is Catalonia's noble and individual version.

Serves 6

200 g/7 oz/7 oz chick-peas, soaked overnight
250 g/9 oz/9 oz breast of veal, cut in two
1 hock of pork
250 g/9 oz/9 oz stewing fowl, cut into pieces
250 g/9 oz/9 oz belly of pork, cut in two lengthwise
2 pig's trotters
200 g/7 oz/7 oz minced pork
2 cloves of garlic, chopped
2 × 15 ml spoons/2 tbsp/2 tbsp flat-leaved parsley, chopped
1 beaten egg
50 g/2 oz/½ cup ground almonds
50 g/2 oz/½ cup fresh breadcrumbs
flour for dusting
250 g/9 oz/9 oz *botifarra blanca* (*see* p.188), in 1 piece
250 g/9 oz/9 oz *botifarra negra* (*see* p.188), in 1 piece
2 large carrots, peeled and julienned
1 celery heart, in strips
200 g/7 oz/7 oz small peeled potatoes
1 small curly cabbage, cut up
salt and freshly ground pepper
200 g/7 oz/7 oz pasta rings (use *galets* in Catalonia)

Pour 4 litres (7 pints) of salted water into a large stewing pot. Bring it slowly to the boil and then add the chick-peas in a muslin bag (so that they do not disintegrate during cooking), the veal, hock of pork, fowl, belly of pork and pig's trotters. Skim at intervals until any scum has been removed, then cover and simmer slowly for 2 hours.

Meanwhile, mix together the minced pork, garlic, parsley, beaten egg, ground almonds and breadcrumbs. Season and with the hands shape six *pilotes* (forcemeat balls) like small round fishcakes, dusting them with flour. Now transfer enough of the broth from the stewpot to a small saucepan to cover the meatballs and simmer for 20 minutes. Remove them, reserve and keep warm, and return the broth to the stewpot.

After the 2 hours' simmering, add to the stewpot the pricked *botifarras*, carrots and celery. Season with salt and pepper and cook for 20 minutes more until all is very tender.

While the last of the ingredients are cooking, transfer a little more of the broth from the stewpot to another saucepan and boil the potatoes and cabbage for 20 minutes, seasoning them with salt and pepper. While preparing the meat and vegetables for serving, make the soup by straining the broth left in the stewpot and boiling the pasta in it for 10 minutes.

Serve the different components of the *escudela* separately as follows:

1. The soup in a tureen.

2. The *pilotes* and the different meats arranged in rows according to type in a large oval dish.

3. The chick-peas and different sorts of vegetable, again arranged in rows in another oval dish.

POSTRES (DESSERTS)

Crema catalana (Baked custard with brittle caramel)

A version of the *flan de huevos* popular all over Spain, this is perhaps the best-known of Catalan desserts.
Serves 6

6 egg yolks, beaten
25 g/1 oz/3 tbsp cornflour
175 g/6 oz/1½ cups icing sugar
500 ml/17 fl oz/2¼ cups milk
1 cinnamon stick
rind of 1 lemon
2 × 15 ml spoons/2 tbsp/2 tbsp brown sugar

Put the egg yolks in a bowl with the cornflour and icing sugar. Simmer the milk with the cinnamon stick and lemon rind, then add the egg mixture and cook slowly to avoid lumps until the custard thickens – do not boil it. This may be done in a large double boiler or in a saucepan placed in a larger pan of boiling water. Remove the cinnamon stick and lemon rind, divide the custard between 6 × 7.5 cm (3 inch) ramekins, and leave to cool in the refrigerator overnight.

Before serving, sprinkle the top with brown sugar and leave for a few seconds under a hot grill, then cool again. Do this about 30 minutes beforehand so that the caramel remains crisp.

In Catalonia, the sugar is caramelized with a salamander (*salamander*) heated on a brazier or ring. This is obtainable in specialized shops in the UK and USA.

Mel i mató

This is a bowl of plain cottage cheese, served with honey on top and sometimes with chopped roasted hazelnuts.

Panellets (Petit fours)

A form of marzipan traditionally eaten on *Los Santos* (All Saints' Day) and accompanied by the sherry-like *vi ranci* (*see* p.167).
Makes approx 1 kg (2 lb)

> *Basic marzipan*
> 450 g/1 lb/2 cups caster sugar
> 125 ml/4½ fl oz/½ cup water
> pinch of cream of tartar
> 450 g/1 lb/3 cups almonds, blanched, skinned, dried and
>   ground (can be done in a food processor)
> 3 eggs

Make a hard ball syrup with the sugar, water and cream of tartar, heating it at 119°C–122°C (245°F–250°F).
   Put the ground almonds into a large bowl and pour the syrup over them very slowly, mixing all the time with a spatula or wooden spoon until smooth and well blended. Now slowly add the 3 unbeaten eggs and continue to mix until the mixture is very smooth. Pour onto a marble slab and leave to cool for about 10 minutes, then work it with the hands for another 10 minutes. It is now ready to use.

Panellets amb pinyons (Panellets with pine kernels)

Take small portions of the basic panellet dough and shape in the hands like walnuts. Paint with unbeaten egg white. Stick pine kernels on top and bake in a moderate oven (180°C, 350°F, Gas 4) for about 10 minutes until the kernels are browned.

Panellets amb llimona (Lemon panellets)

These are made in the same way as *panellets amb pinyons*, but lemon rind is substituted for the pine kernels.

Postre de music (Busker's delight)

This is simply a mixture of the nuts which grow so plentifully in Catalonia – walnuts, hazelnuts, pine kernels etc. – with dried fruits such as raisins and figs. The name stems from the time when itinerant musicians toured the countryside and were fed for their pains, the mixture of nuts being the reward for a particularly spirited performance.

Refresc de menta (Mint sorbet)

This recipe was the creation of Josep Mercader of the then Motel Ampurdán and is reproduced by courtesy of his son-in-law and successor at the Hotel-Restaurant Ampurdán, Jaume Subirós. Sr Subirós has recently devised another delicious sorbet, using thyme flowers in the spring. It is made in the same way by infusing the pink flowers in water.

> 100 g/4 oz/½ cup caster sugar
> large bunch of mint leaves, well-washed
> a few sprigs of mint for decoration
> ½ litre/1 pint/2 cups fresh lemon juice

Bring to the boil 1 litre/2 pints/4 cups of water with the sugar in a saucepan, then add the mint and simmer for 8 to 10 minutes. Chill in the refrigerator overnight and next morning strain the syrup and discard the mint. Add the lemon juice and stir in well.

Transfer to an ice cream maker and follow the instructions.

Taronjas a la cava (Oranges with cava)

This recipe is from the excellent Casa Irene in the mountain resort of Arties in the Pyrenees.
Serves 6

> 6 oranges
> 1 bottle brut cava
> 225 ml/8 fl oz/1 cup water
> 350 g/12 oz/1½ cups sugar
> few drops Campari

Peel the oranges. Cut the rind into strips and reserve. Put the water, cava, sugar and Campari into a pan and bring to the boil. Add the oranges and when they begin to blanch, add the orange peel and continue cooking for 5 to 8 minutes. Now remove the oranges and place them in a glass bowl. Reduce the liquid, adding a little more Campari if desired.

Pour the reduced liquid over the oranges, cool, refrigerate and serve.

Further reading

Andrews, Coleman *Catalan Cuisine*, London 1989

Descharnes, Robert *Gaudí, The Visionary*, new edn, London 1982

Ford, Richard *A Handbook for Travellers in Spain*, 1845, reprinted Centaur Press, London 1966. *Gatherings from Spain*, London 1846, reprinted Dent, London 1970

Hare, Augustus *Wanderings in Spain*, London 1873

Lewis, Norman *Voices of the Old Sea*, London 1984 and in paperback

Llibre de Sent Soví (14C and 15C Catalan recipes), trans. Rudolf Grew, Barcelona 1979

Macaulay, Rose *Fabled Shore*, London 1949 and later paperback edns

Manjón, Maite *Gastronomy of Spain and Portugal*, London 1990

Orwell, George *Homage to Catalonia*, London 1952 and in paperback

Read, Jan *The Catalans*, London 1978. *The Wines of Spain*, 2nd edn, London 1986. *Pocket Guide to Spanish Wines*, 2nd edn, London 1988

Rubert de Nola *Libro de Guisados, Manjares y Potages*, Valladolid edn of 1529, reprinted Editorial Artes Graficas, Madrid-Palma de Mallorca 1968

Torres, Miguel A. *Manual de los vinos de Cataluña*, Madrid 1982. *The Distinctive Wines of Catalonia*, Barcelona 1986. *Mil Años de Viticultura en Cataluña* (with English translation), Barcelona 1990

Torres, Marimar *The Spanish Table*, London 1987

Trueta, J. *The Spirit of Catalonia*, Oxford 1946

Vicens, Vives *Approaches to the History of Spain*, Berkeley 1967

For a comprehensive bibliography of more specialized books in Catalan, Spanish and English, interested readers are referred to *The Catalans* by Jan Read, listed above.

The Department de Comerç, Consum i Turisme issues a series of informative and well-illustrated pamphlets on natural parks, wildlife and outdoor activities, obtainable free from tourist offices.

The red *Michelin Guide to Spain and Portugal* is recommended for its detailed lists of hotels and restaurants, and town plans.

Index

Numbers in italics refer to illustrations